And I

Always Wil

For Renee,

My inspiration... My imagination…
My determination... My stimulation...
My love!

george@georgehathaway.com

Published in the United States by POV Publications
info@POVpubs.com

ISBN-13: 978-0-578-20066-8
ISBN-10: 057820066X

Printed in the United States of America

1

The Funeral

The hearse moved slowly along Mount Vernon Road.

It then turned through the gates of the Maine Veterans Memorial Cemetery. The broad, grassy slopes, were dotted with oak, maple, and pine. It provided an honorable resting place for those who had served. Its simple beauty and lingering tenderness reminded visitors of Arlington.

The July shower spread its glaze across the headstones and nameplates sunken in the grass. They were all perfectly aligned, as required to be.

Each departed veteran was honored with an American flag attached to a small, wooden stanchion set perfectly vertical in the ground and correctly positioned close to its marker. Thousands of small, star-spangled banners hung in the calm, morning wetness honoring the sacrifice the brave men and women gave in service to their country.

The hearse pulled to a stop at the entrance to the marble, committal chapel.

It was a solemn place, befitting the deep respect paid to all veterans who passed through to their final resting place.

The rain forced the ceremony inside.

The funeral procession behind the hearse consisted of over fifty cars. One by one each vehicle stopped. Umbrellas burst open against the rain.

Riley and Charlie Thurman got out of their car and waited for Riley's two daughters as they pulled in behind them. Kelly and Lauren got out and quickly caught up.

Riley's face was covered in tears. It couldn't be helped. Sunglasses were of no use. It was silly, of course. It was raining. Who was she fooling? Most of the other women were wearing them, too.

Riley's daughters were not.

Owen's death was expected, but that didn't matter anymore. Riley's despair had been deep for a long time. She didn't know how she could live without him. He was so easy to love. Living with him was vivid, full of flowers and rainbows. It was pure joy and more intimate than one could imagine. Owen made life easy to live. All her needs and desires had fallen together in his arms.

Riley promised herself that she would hide her grief, especially from her daughters. She wanted to be strong, but the ache was deep in her soul.

As they neared the chapel, she struggled to keep from thinking about the bad times, too. The pain of those memories washed across her eyes.

The four of them walked together, surrounded by mourners. Riley held hands with both Charlie and Lauren. Her tears continued to flow, but he couldn't tell through her glasses.

The honor guard of six Army soldiers, in their dress blues, marched in two columns to the back of the hearse. They opened its rear door. In silence, one small step at a time, they slid the casket slowly out of the hearse and awaited their command.

Colonel Vance, the detail's commanding officer, stood behind the casket. With precise, well-coordinated steps, she followed her team as they slowly marched the flag-draped casket through the chapel doors.

Once inside, the detail continued to move at attention to the back of the chapel and placed the casket on a covered, metal gurney.

Riley, Charlie, and the girls entered with the others.

The greeting on the placard just inside read, "*Owen Stewart Flynn, Colonel, United States Army (retired).*"

Riley paused to read the sign then took a long, slow breath. Flashes of so many good times spun through her head. Sandy beaches, sailing, the pool, the love codes, Boston, *Airship*, and the back seat of Owen's car were just a few powerful memories that brightened her thoughts, if only for a moment.

The honor guard remained at attention until all were seated. Colonel Vance quietly ordered her men to move the casket to the front of the chapel. When finished, they sat in their reserved, front row seats.

An Army chaplain stepped to the microphone, "Please stand and bow your head."

He delivered a brief prayer then asked the visitors to be seated.

In his dress blue uniform, Brigadier General Jordan Hitchcock stepped onto the platform and replaced the chaplain at the podium.

Hitchcock began, "Ladies and gentlemen, thank you all for being here today to honor one of Maine's most courageous, native sons. Colonel Owen Stewart Flynn was loved by everyone who knew him as a strong, decent, and honorable man who worked diligently to make his community exceptional."

He went on to tell of Owen's twenty years of service in the United States Army, his two years in Vietnam flying Huey Gunships, the wounds he suffered, and the many awards he received in combat.

Hitchcock added, "Owen's love of flying was persistent. So, after the Army, he spent another twenty years as a commercial pilot and executive for United Airlines.

Yet, after all of these accomplishments, he would tell you that his greatest legacy were his three children, Colleen, Evan, and Sean along with his five grandchildren, all of whom are with us today.

Throughout his later years, you all knew him as an active community leader down the road in Kennebunkport. He was also an avid sailor right up until just a few days ago when it was time for him to leave us. He was a young seventy-year-old when he passed. The war had caught up with him.

We will all miss him very much.

The honor guard will now fold and present the flag."

Colonel Vance ordered, "Present h'arms!" All in attendance stood at their chairs.

The honor guard sharply moved to either side of the casket. They stood at attention awaiting their command.

Vance signaled the Army rifle team to begin their 21-gun salute.

The honor guard picked up the flag and held it taught just above the casket. Colonel Vance rendered her salute at the out-stretched flag before her.

Outside the chapel, the rifle team stood among the white grave markers. Together, the seven Army soldiers raised their rifles to the sky, loaded a blank round into the chamber, and prepared to fire the traditional three volleys.

Across the still wetness, the crack of the guns startled the mourners inside, "Ready... fire. Ready... fire. Ready... fire."

Immediately after the twenty-one-gun salute, a lone Army bugler stood at attention away from the rifle squad, raised a bugle to his lips, and sounded Taps.

Vance then ordered her detail to fold the flag. In precise movements, representing America's thirteen original colonies, they folded the flag thirteen times into the shape of an eighteenth-century tricorne hat.

When she received the flag, she saluted the soldier who had just handed it to her. She placed it on top of the outstretched palm of her left hand. She was handed three empty shell casings from the rifle team and inserted them into the folds of the flag. She placed her right hand over the top of the flag to ensure a firm hold.

She performed a 'smart' about-face, took two steps forward, and bent down on one knee to present the flag to Colleen, Owen's next of kin, seated in the front row.

Vance concentrated on Colleen's eyes and quietly spoke to her, "On behalf of the President of the United States, the United States Army, and a grateful nation, please accept this flag as a symbol of their appreciation for your loved one's honorable and faithful service."

The colonel passed the flag to Colleen, who softly thanked her and placed it on her lap.

Vance straightened back to attention, again saluted, and commanded, "Order... h'arms."

After the colonel's team rendered their salutes, the chaplain, Vance, and the honor guard marched out of the chapel.

Back at the podium, Hitchcock concluded the service, "I'd like to thank all of you, again, for coming today to help celebrate the life of an extraordinary man and a genuine hero. May I invite each of you to rise and take the opportunity to say your goodbyes to Colonel Flynn."

He stepped off the podium and shook the hand of each member of Owen's family. He quietly exited the ceremony.

Owen's daughter and two sons, his grandchildren, and several other close relatives stood and lined up to the left of the casket. The guests began their move to the front. Owen's family greeted each of them as they passed.

The line of mourners was long, and their goodbyes took considerable time. Lauren and Kelly stayed seated.

When Riley finally reached the casket, she stopped to softly rest her hand on the closed case. Through her fingertips she sensed the love and passion she felt from the simple, soft touch of Owen's hand. Every moment they shared passed across her eyes. Every dream they wished flashed through her mind. Every pain they endured darkened her soul.

She bowed her head crying. She could hardly move. Charlie put an arm over her shoulder and lowered his head in prayer.

After what seemed an eternity, he whispered to her, "Sweetheart, we should let others have their turn."

She nodded in agreement. But then, before moving away, she bent toward the casket and kissed it.

Ensuring no one heard her words, she whispered to Owen, "My love, I miss you so very much. 3-1-6-3."

When Riley turned to step away from the casket, Colleen reached out to her. In tears, they hugged each other.

After a few seconds, Colleen pulled back, "Riley, I'm so sorry. This is such a difficult day for all of us. I know it's even more so for you. My Dad loved you so very deeply and so completely. You were all he talked about when you were together, more so after you left."

"Thank you, Colleen. It means a lot to me that you care so much."

"Of course I care about you. Because of you, my father stayed young at heart and so happy to be alive. We all could see it. As Dad requested, I'm giving you one of his Army dog tags. The other one is with him now."

She handed it to Riley, who kissed it, and closed her fingers around it.

She could not stop her tears as she tried to tell Colleen, "Thank you for this. I know how very much the Army meant to him. I'll never let go of it."

Colleen nodded her acceptance.

Riley added, "You were so good to him. I know you understand why I had to go. You know better than anyone how ill he became. He was convinced it had something to do with his time in Vietnam. He pleaded with me to leave. I stayed as long as I could. He was the love of my life."

"You should never worry about leaving Dad when you did. Only the hospital could give him the care he needed. And, I know he wanted you to get on with your life. He was very persistent, as I recall."

Riley smiled, "That he was, Colleen. I cry every day. I miss him so much. He was so proud of you and your family. He was a really great human being, and we're all very fortunate to have been a small part of his life. I wish the very best for you and your family."

As she started to move away, Colleen took hold of Riley's hand, "I wish the very best for you, too. I know that's what Dad would want, as well."

Then, she bent forward and took time to say something into Riley's ear.

When finished, she straightened up and told Riley, "Stay safe."

Riley smiled at the comment, "You, too, Colleen. Stay safe, as well."

As they moved on past the family members, Charlie asked her, "What did she just whisper to you?"

In an effort to avoid answering his question, she lied to him, "Uh. Well. I'm not really sure what she said. It's so noisy in here."

Riley and Charlie reached the back of the chapel. The girls met up with them at the door.

Lauren hugged her mother, "Mom, we're going to go on home now. Are you going to be okay?"

"Yes, thanks, Lauren. And, thanks to both of you for coming today. I know how difficult it must have been for you. I love you, both."

The girls kissed their mother, waved to Charlie, and headed to their car.

Before they left the building, Riley stopped to look back at the casket. It was the last time she would ever see Owen. The love of her life was gone. She bowed her head, crying again.

Charlie wrapped his arms around her and held onto her.

She looked into his eyes, "I have to tell you something. When Owen and I were together, he joked that I would find a man named Charlie who would take good care of me. Then he made me promise that I would tell you about us."

Charlie looked hard at her, "Am I going to have a problem with this?"

"Not at all. In fact, I think you're going to be surprised at what you hear. This is going to take a while so let's sit down."

They moved to a damp bench outside the entrance to the chapel.

Riley began their story, "My friendship with Owen started on a rainy, June afternoon eight years ago. And, you're right, we became much more than just friends. Together we found love like never before. He made me incredibly happy. In fact, happier than I'd ever been. He took good care of me and made sure I was always safe. He opened my eyes to what life is really all about. We trusted and respected each other completely. He helped me believe in myself for the very first time. He was fun, and he made me laugh all the time. He was an honest, wonderful friend, and, yes, an affectionate lover.

And, everyone in my family wanted him dead."

2

The Haircut

Eight years earlier...

Owen Flynn hadn't seen so much rain in a long time. But, on that day, it was hitting hard and driving in it was more than a challenge.

He'd left his office in Portland ten minutes earlier traveling south on the Maine Turnpike. His windshield wipers were set to high speed, but the rain was winning the battle. He was doing the best he could as he made his way back to Kennebunkport.

Nearing town, he turned off Port Road onto Western Avenue. After he crossed the Kennebunk River, he passed the local shops and entered the parking lot behind Alisson's Restaurant.

Before he exited his car, he took off his suitcoat, put on his foul weather jacket, and replaced his dress shoes and socks with Topsiders. Of course, no respectable sailor would wear socks.

The rain continued to pour down on Owen as he raced across the parking lot and up the alley between Dock Square Clothiers and the Looking Glass Salon. He turned and immediately entered the salon. Inside, he shook the rain off his clothes.

He was right on time and not surprised to see that the salon was full of women. Many of them took notice of his arrival.

Owen was a handsome, sixty-two-year-old. Most people who met him guessed him to be much younger. His silver-gray hair was thick and full. His eyes were green, bright, and clear. Light wrinkles crisscrossed his tanned face. The dimple in his chin was surrounded by a neatly-trimmed beard. His smile was infectious.

As he stepped to the counter, a rather attractive woman moved from the back of the salon to greet him. She was smiling broadly.

She extended her hand to him, "Good evening, sir. I'm Riley Reed. Do you have an appointment with us today?"

He reached across the counter and shook her hand, "Yes, I'm Owen Flynn. I called the other day for a six o'clock appointment."

She continued her smile as she looked down at the day's schedule next to the cash register, "Yes, Mr. Flynn. Here you are. Crystal Sands is going to take care of you today. I think you'll like her. So, let's get you started. Shall we?"

Moments earlier, Crystal had finished with another client and was sweeping up the clippings on the floor around her chair.

Riley interrupted her, "Crystal? This is Owen Flynn. I mentioned to you yesterday that he was going to be a new client of yours."

They shook hands as Crystal smiled, "So very nice to meet you, sir."

"Please. No need to be formal with me. I'm just Owen. Is your name really Crystal Sands?"

Riley answered for her, "Everyone asks her that. And, yes, it really is her name."

Crystal shrugged her shoulders, "Okay, now that we've gotten over the intro's, please have a seat."

Riley stayed and leaned against Crystal's station.

After he sat down, Crystal joked, "I hope I do okay with your hair today. This is my first day on the job, ya' know?"

He nodded and snapped right back, "That's all right. This is my first haircut. So, this should be a win-win for both of us."

The three of them laughed as Crystal wrapped her stylist cape over him and secured it with two snaps at the back of his neck.

She needed to get some product out of her supply cabinet, "Will you excuse me for a minute? I'll be right back."

With Crystal out of earshot, Riley told Owen, "I think you'll find her to be a lot of fun. Her sense of humor is a little crazy at times, but a lot of fun. I'll head back to my desk now and put your head in her hands... literally."

He stopped her, "By the way, do you cut hair, too?"

"No, I don't do hair anymore. When I'm not running the shop, I take care of peoples' nails. You know, manicures and pedicures? You should try me sometime. I promise you'll enjoy it."

She headed for the back of the salon.

Owen couldn't help but stare at Riley. Her face was perfection, and her deep, brown eyes seemed to smile with every word she spoke. She was well-tanned and tall, maybe five feet ten. She wore a bright, colorful sundress that highlighted her best features. Her waist was narrow, her hips were perfectly proportioned, and her blonde hair hung softly across her shoulders. She had long arms with elegant hands and graceful fingers.

"I think I've just met the most beautiful woman I've ever seen."

But, there was something in her voice that betrayed a problem. He couldn't put his finger on it, so he dismissed the thought for the time being.

Crystal returned and discovered Owen in a daze as he watched Riley walk back to her desk.

She bent down and quietly interrupted him, "Isn't she just beautiful? We all love her."

A bit embarrassed, he returned from his trance, "Sorry, Crystal. I guess you're right. Yes, she's very nice."

"Now that I have you back on earth, what would you like me to do today?"

"Let's try it short in the back, but mostly thinned out. Both of my grandfathers died with a thick head of hair. So, be careful with it. It's inherited."

She smiled at his joke then ran her fingers through his hair, "Ha... You're very lucky. It feels great."

He glanced, again, across the salon at Riley. He couldn't help but be surprised that she was smiling at him. He had no choice, but to smile back.

Riley was pleased to see that Owen was smiling at her. She liked what she saw. She wondered how old he might be. Fifty? Fifty-two? It was hard to tell. He wasn't that tall, but his posture made him seem so. He was well-tanned and obviously spent a lot of time out in the sun. The dimple in his chin and his graying beard were cute and, along with his smile, oddly stimulating.

She liked the way he dressed, too. After he hung up his jacket, she saw a crisp, white, button-down dress shirt, a maroon and gold striped tie, and dark-gray suit pants. She figured that he had just come from work somewhere.

It appeared to her that he didn't wrinkle.

Crystal planned to spend about forty minutes cutting his hair. Normally it would take her only about twenty minutes, but she wanted him in her chair for as long as she could get away with it.

"So, how did you hear about our salon?"

"My wife told me she'd heard good things from some friends who'd been here recently. I was looking for a new barber anyway, so it seemed a good idea to give you a try."

"Well, I for one am very happy that you did. I hope I do a good job for you."

"Oh, I'm sure you will. Don't worry about it."

She began to trim the back of his head, "So, do you live here in Kennebunkport?"

"Yes, I was born up in Portland. My family had a summer home here while I was growing up. It's my year-round home now."

"So, I suppose your house is one of those big ones on the water?"

"Actually, it is. We're over on Windemere, with a rocky beach that we just can't use."

Feeling she'd made a mistake, she apologized, "Oh, I'm so sorry. I shouldn't have tried to be cute about where you live."

"Don't worry. My family's been a big part of this town going back hundreds of years. I got used to the ribbing thing when I was still young."

"Okay, I won't ask any more family history questions. How about your work? What do you do for a living?"

"I work for United Airlines at the airport up in Portland. I was a commercial pilot with United for quite a while before landing a desk job there. I still fly... my boat, that is."

Crystal's eyebrows jumped, "You have a boat? Is it sail or power?"

"Do I look like I drive a stinkpot? No way. I'm a sailor!"

Riley walked up to them, stopped in front of Owen, and leaned against Crystal's work station, again.

It was obvious she wanted to join the conversation, "I couldn't help but overhear the two of you talking about sailing. Do you have your own boat, Owen?"

"Yes, I sure do. It's a forty-two-foot J/Boat. Her name is *Airship*."

"I'd love to see it. Do you have a photo?"

"Sorry. No, I don't right now. I'll bring one to my next haircut."

"Do you park it near here?"

He chuckled a bit, "Yes, she's tied up at the Arundel Yacht Club off Ocean Avenue."

"Crystal and I should surprise you there someday."

He looked up at Riley, "That would be fun. I'd enjoy showing the two of you the ropes."

Riley saw a familiar face come through the door, "Enough small talk. My next client has just arrived, so I need to get back to work."

Before she left, she glanced at Owen's ring finger and felt oddly disappointed that he was married. She patted him on the shoulder then headed back to her manicure desk.

Crystal continued to chat about sailing, local events, gossip, and the weather. He enjoyed talking and listening to her. She had a wonderful sense of humor that made him laugh often.

Still, he took every chance he could to glance over at Riley and wonder what she was thinking.

Crystal finished, "There you are, Owen. How'd I do?"

She moved her hand mirror behind him so he could see the back of his head.

He ran his fingers through his hair and was pleased to find how well she'd thinned it out, "Thanks, Crystal... This is great!"

"I'm glad you like it. Might we see you again, then?"

"Of course. How about in two weeks? Can I make an appointment with you now?"

Crystal opened her book, "Let's see what I have. Do you want to do Friday the fifteenth at six again?"

"That's excellent, thanks. I'll need an appointment card. I'm just terrible at remembering appointments without a card."

After she handed him the card, he started for the door.

From the back of the salon, Riley called to him, "Goodbye, Owen. Nice to meet you, sir."

He turned to see her smiling at him as she quickly waved goodbye.

He smiled and waved back at her.

Ella McKenna, Riley's sister, was also a stylist at the salon. She couldn't help but notice that Riley appeared to be more than casually interested in the salon's newest customer. Was Riley flirting with him? She pushed the question out of her head and returned to coloring her client's hair.

She decided that she'd think more about it later.

3

The Dinner

Before returning to his car, Owen stopped at O'Malley's Market.

He loved the taste of fresh spinach and decided to have some at dinner with his wife later that night. He picked out a couple of choice filets, a considerable bunch of spinach, and two healthy, baking potatoes. Before he checked out, he selected a special bottle of merlot to go with the meal.

By the time he got home that evening, it was 7:30. His longhaired Dachshund, Zeke, greeted him at the kitchen door and kept bumping his nose against Owen's right heel. He laughed at his dog's persistence to greet him that way every day. They both loved it.

He stopped at the refrigerator and placed the steak and spinach on the top shelf. The potatoes landed on the counter to wait their turn on the grill. He next pulled out a Shipyard Summer Ale, popped the cap, and walked out to the back deck. After wiping off the remnants of the rain from his favorite deck chair, he sat down and began working on his beer.

Zeke followed him and laid down in front of his master's chair. There, he dropped his favorite dirty tennis ball at Owen's feet. A sense of anticipation was deep in Zeke's eyes, waiting patiently, as he kept gawking at the ball.

Owen couldn't let him down. He picked up the ball and threw it long across the back yard. Zeke spun around, bounced his short legs down the three steps to the lawn, and chased after the ball. Owen knew that Zeke would return to repeat the game a few moments later.

As he looked across the back lawn and out at the ocean in front of him, the sparkle of the sinking sun off the water made him think of Riley, *"Is it my imagination or was she smiling at me all the time I was in her shop? No. It's not possible."*

Meeting Riley at the salon made him somewhat nervous, yet he liked the feeling she gave him. He knew it was wrong to have such thoughts. He felt a bit guilty but continued them anyway.

A few minutes later, Julie entered the driveway and parked her car in front of the garage. She pulled two bags of groceries from the back seat and went into the house.

She looked out of the kitchen window and saw her husband on the back deck.

She walked over to the screen door and spoke through it, "How'd your haircut go?"

Owen got up and called Zeke to join him in the kitchen.

On the way, he answered her, "Okay, I guess. A lot of women were there. I was the only man in the whole place."

"Is that a problem?"

"Nope. Not at all."

She checked his haircut, "It looks like they cut it too short in the back."

"Well, it'll grow back just fine. By the way, on my way home I picked up some steaks for dinner tonight, and..."

"What? I just came from the grocery store with tonight's dinner. I told you we're having chicken. Remember?"

Owen dropped his head, "I forgot. I'm sorry. We'll just have the steaks tomorrow night instead."

She screamed at him, "No, we're not! We're going to dinner tomorrow at the Holcomb's. Or, did you forget that, too? Jesus, Owen! It seems like you're forgetting things more and more every day. What's your problem?"

He was frustrated that his wife had become more difficult to deal with. He wasn't sure how to handle her. He believed that, yes, he forgot about dinner at the Holcomb's, but it wasn't a catastrophe deserving of a tongue lashing from his wife. There was a time when their love for each other softened every mistake.

He lifted his head to face her and tried to recover, "Look. I said I was sorry. I'm not having any problems. I just..."

She interrupted him again, "This is about me, isn't it? You don't listen to me anymore. Why, Owen? Tell me why!"

Julie found herself to be less and less a partner in their marriage. Owen was only the second love of her life. Many years ago, she was in love with Jeremy Thompson, a local boy she first met in high school. They dated a long time, and everyone predicted they'd marry someday.

But, Jeremy got drunk one night out on a binge with friends and lost control of his car. He was killed instantly. Julie had been emotionally disabled ever since. She hated herself for not trying harder to keep him from going out that night. Still, she blamed herself for his death. She loved Jeremy, even more than her own husband.

Owen didn't have an answer for Julie's flare-up. He just bent his head back down again and turned away.

While pointing a finger at his back, she yelled at him again, "All you're really doing is pretending that I matter to you. If you were still in love with me, you'd accept my criticisms and not dismiss them the way you do."

He continued his silence.

Disgusted, she gave up and spewed her grocery bags across the counter. She pivoted and ran up to the bedroom, leaving Owen to clean up the mess.

After he put the groceries away, he grabbed another Shipyard from the refrigerator and returned to his chair on the deck. He sat back and bent his head down.

Zeke assumed his favorite spot at Owen's feet. The dog had walked off the deck when Julie started yelling at his master.

Owen thought to himself, *"Welcome home, my dear. I'm happy to see you, too."*

4

The Airship

A week later, Owen had plans to sail down to Perkins Cove.

He was anxious to meet up with Bill Stafford. Bill was not only his best friend, but also the man in charge of the foredeck during their yacht races.

Owen's internal clock woke him every morning at 6:00, and that day was no exception.

Julie was sound asleep when he quietly got out of bed, showered, and dressed for a day of solo sailing.

Zeke followed him down to the kitchen and sat waiting for him. As usual, Owen knew that Zeke wouldn't need a leash when he opened the door to the porch.

They walked across the backyard and headed for the water. It was early still, and the tide was out. The rising sun was warming the air.

Zeke remained at heel. When Owen stopped, the dog looked up, as if to seek permission to chase the Sandpipers along the water's edge. Owen smiled at him and gave him just a simple nod. With the signal, Zeke was off after his target. He knew he'd not catch a single bird. It was only the chase that mattered.

After a half-hour of Zeke racing after the birds and splashing through the shallow waves, Owen whistled to him. Zeke returned up through the rocks, across the grass, and onto the back porch. Owen followed and fell into his deckchair, looking out to sea.

With Zeke laying at his feet, Owen pondered his deepening problems with Julie. Their marriage had been deteriorating for years, and he was at a loss to repair the damage that'd been done. Maybe their relationship had become boring. Maybe, after the kids were born, the love and affection they once shared had overgrown with time. They were no longer in touch with each other, and the emotions between them had become bitter.

There would be enough energy, later, to further examine their marriage. But, now, it was time to go sailing.

Owen put on his Topsiders and yellow foul weather jacket then took the boat keys off the wall hook. He let Zeke in off the deck then exited and locked the door behind him.

It was a seven-minute drive to the yacht club and *Airship*. Owen parked his Jeep in his favorite spot. He got out, opened the rear cargo door, and grabbed his gear. He closed up the car.

He walked to the end of the dock where *Airship* was waiting. He stepped through the port boarding gate onto her deck, jumped into the cockpit, and unlocked the hatch to the galley below.

Airship was a stunning, forty-two-foot sailboat with a fifty-foot mast. She had every technology an airline pilot could ever want in a boat. Besides the shortwave ship-to-shore radio, her radar system was fully integrated with GPS navigation. In addition, her instruments included a chart plotter, sonar array, and weather-fax. Most instruments had video displays. The boom and mast provided for powered furling and reefing of the mainsail from controls in the cockpit. On the foredeck, she also had a roller, furling jib.

All in all, Owen could sail her around the world by himself if he wanted to. But, while on this trip to Perkins Cove, he just wanted to enjoy playing with the controls to see if he could break his own speed record.

He reached up to the cover over the main and pulled the ties from around it. He dragged the cover through the open hatch. Once in the cabin below, he folded the cover and threw it behind the aft bulkhead. Then he turned on the circuit breakers and checked the battery power.

He returned topside and watched as the electronics came to life. He then checked the fuel level to be certain he could rely on the engine in case *Airship* was becalmed.

Owen set the throttle to 'Neutral' and inserted the ignition key. He started the engine and checked that the bilge pump was operating normally.

Airship was nearly ready to leave the dock.

He picked up the ship-to-shore radio and selected the proper channel.

Then he clicked the push-to-talk button and called the Coast Guard for a radio check, "South Portland Coast Guard, this is *Airship* out of Kennebunk-port. Radio check, please. Over."

A Coastie clicked in almost immediately and responded, "*Airship*, I read you five-by-five. Let us know when you're underway, sir. Over."

"Roger that. Thanks. Over and out."

The cockpit displays and indicators showed that the engine and electronics were operating properly.

Owen returned below, grabbed his life vest from behind the bulkhead, and slung it over his shoulder. He left the cabin, got back into the cockpit, and closed the hatch. He strapped his life vest on.

Owen tied off the mooring lines and pushed the boat away from the dock. He turned the helm five degrees to starboard and eased the throttle 'Forward.'

Airship was underway.

After she cleared the dock, Owen steered her out into the Kennebunk River. With all the other boats around him, *Airship's* speed had to be kept just short of producing a wake.

After several minutes, *Airship* passed between the jetties at the mouth of the river. He increased the throttle as he prepared to head into open water.

Once past the jetties, and with no other boats close by, he slowed the engine and adjusted the helm forty-five degrees to port putting the wind directly over her bow. He moved out of the cockpit to pull in the rubber fenders hanging over the port side.

It was time for *Airship* to set sail.

He turned the sail controls on and powered the main to the top of the mast. Next, he unfurled the jib on the forestay.

He steered to a southwest heading. The offshore breeze was now flowing over the starboard quarter, so he set both sails to port for a broad reach, starboard tack.

Finally, he turned the engine off which folded the propeller blades to reduce drag.

His plan was to arrive at Perkins Cove for an early lunch with Bill. The steady wind and calm seas told him he was sure to arrive on time.

He grabbed the radio mic and, again, opened the channel to the Coast Guard, "South Portland Coast Guard, this is *Airship* out of Kennebunkport. Heading southwest at six knots. Destination is Perkins Cove. Over."

"*Airship*, South Portland Coast Guard. Your course is clear and the weather is fair. Wind is out of the northwest at ten knots with gusts up to twelve. Seas are less than two feet. Be safe and have a good sail, sir. Over."

"Roger that. I'll let you know when I arrive. Thank you. Over and out."

Owen spent a few minutes making adjustments to the helm and the sails. His objective was to ensure that the tell-tails on the sails were all flying straight back, ensuring he got the most speed he could from the wind.

This was the best part of sailing. Alone, surrounded by the ocean's beauty, cruising with a 'lady' he loved, and pretty much in control of everything.

He'd be leaving home far behind today but would miss his dog.

The trip from Kennebunkport to Perkins Cove in Ogunquit was a short one by sea. Given good weather and the right wind, sailing there could take about an hour. By car it was only about twelve miles. But, driving there was not nearly as much fun as sailing there. Every time he made the trip, Owen tried to set a new, personal speed record. This day would be no exception.

Airship's clock read 10:15.

With a steady, northwest breeze, the water was not very choppy. He knew he'd have to keep the helm slightly to starboard most of the way. He turned to his navigation system, set his course for Perkins Cove, and started the timer. It was pretty much a straight shot, and, with a steady breeze, he smiled knowing that he'd make the trip without tacking or jibing even once.

He pulled down on the boom vang then tugged at the downhaul to get the main as flat as possible. He let the main out just a little until her tell-tails were straight back. He adjusted the jib sheet so its tell-tails were flying as close to horizontal as possible, too.

Airship was designed for both cruising and racing. Owen loved adjusting the controls as if they were the trim tabs on a 737. Her speed reached just over seven knots. Despite the lack of rail-huggers, *Airship* listed only five degrees to port. The Nav' system displayed an estimated time of arrival at 11:15.

Owen was eager to talk with his best friend.

5

The Beach

It was just after 8:00 when Riley got up.

She stayed in her pajamas and headed downstairs.

Every time she walked into her kitchen she was reminded of how pissed off she was that it was as old as the house itself, built in 1935. If she had her way, she'd gut the place and start over with an open format, up-to-date appliances, and stained cherry cabinets with cut-glass pulls. She would put in a comfortable, little, breakfast nook and brighten it all up with more windows.

Yes, her kitchen really sucked. But she couldn't change anything unless Jason, her husband, agreed. And, he wouldn't.

She brewed a pot of coffee, poured a cup, and took it into the living room to watch the news. Except for the weather, she was really not interested in what her television had to tell her.

She looked forward to taking the day off from the salon and spending it at the beach with her best friend, Vivienne Lawler.

She hated doing laundry, but she knew it was down there in the basement calling for her. No, make that screaming for her. She also knew that if she didn't get to it soon, Jason's mother, Caryn, would be stopping by to take charge of just about everything in her house. And, that would include the laundry.

She hated her mother-in-law.

Laundry was one of the many things Caryn tried to control every time she came over. She never did a good job with it, or with anything else, for that matter. And, Riley was always expected to clean up after her.

Yet, Riley was not allowed to comment or complain about Caryn. She was forbidden to say anything critical of his mother. If she did, she knew she'd feel the full force of her husband's fury.

Jason really loved his mother. So much so, that he long-ago adopted her need to control everything around her. He also assumed his mother's belief that she could no wrong. And, just like his mother, he never apologized for anything. He was an unhappy man and labored hard at acquiring his mother's deep contempt for life itself.

Riley descended to the laundry room to start the washer. She pulled the clothes out of the hamper and sorted them into three piles. While she was loading the washer with the dark clothes, Jason came down the stairs in his gray, pinstriped suit.

"Hey, shouldn't you be getting ready to go? We're supposed to be at the church in forty-five minutes!"

Riley placed both hands on the washer lid and slammed it shut, "What're you talking about? What church?"

"What do you mean 'what church?' We have to be at St. Bernard's by eleven for the christening. Tell me you didn't forget!"

She turned to him and planted her fists on her hips, "Christening? I don't know about any christening."

He was immediately pissed off and yelled back at her, "What the fuck is wrong with you? I told you last Monday that my boss's baby was being christened today, and I'm going to be her Godfather. Remember?"

She threw her arms into the air as she stormed past him on her way upstairs, "Jesus, Jase! You never told me that! You do this to me all the time."

He went after her, "So, as usual, you're telling me you just forgot about this ceremony. I know I told you. I even put it in the calendar on the refrigerator."

She entered the kitchen with Jason close behind and went to the calendar stuck to the refrigerator door. She found nothing about a christening.

"There, you dumb ass! Do you see anything about going to church this morning?"

He pushed her out of the way to get a look for himself.

"Shit! Okay, so, I didn't put it in the calendar. So, what? I know I told you. Come on, get dressed, or we'll be late."

Riley didn't budge, "I'm not going!"

"What do you mean you're not going? This is my boss's kid. I'm going to be her Godfather, for Christ sake. You have to be there with me. What'll my boss think if you're not there?"

"I really don't give a shit what your boss will think, Jase. Not one bit. My best advice to you is just tell him you fucked up again and forgot to tell me about it."

He grabbed her forearm and twisted it, "You're a fucking idiot. Why did I ever marry you?"

"I've asked myself that same question for years, now. So, let go of me!"

"If I have to, I'll drag you there myself! You're going with me, and that's that!"

"I told you, no, I'm not going. I already have plans to spend the day at the beach with Viv."

"Viv? That's bullshit, and you know it. She's off in Europe somewhere. You're lying to me again."

She started upstairs and paused to scream over the railing, "No, you moron! She came back two days ago. So, no, I'm not going to be with you. I'm going to be with her."

Jase yelled back, "I don't believe you, you little shit. I don't trust you one bit. I'll bet you're really going off to be with some asshole. Aren't you?"

She ignored the typical nonsense from her husband. She knew she didn't flirt with other men at all. And, she despised him for trying to 'protect' her from some imaginary threat. It seemed that Jase only wanted to protect himself.

Long ago, it had become clear to her that he would never stop treating her with such utter disrespect. But, she couldn't figure out how to stop it.

She entered the bedroom and slammed the door behind her. Still mad as Hell, she changed into her bathing suit and threw her beach bag together. She put on her flip-flops then came back down the stairs into the kitchen. She took two bottles of wine out of the refrigerator then made sandwiches for lunch. She put them in her bag along with chips and snacks for the day.

Jason was pissed off and squirmed while in his chair in the living room.

Fully packed and ready to go, Riley opened the kitchen door to leave for the day.

She yelled back at her husband, "I'm really looking forward to seeing Viv's face when I tell her you just called her an asshole."

She laughed at him when he yelled back, "Fuck you!"

She jumped in her car and sped away from the house. She was happy to leave Jase hanging like that. She got a certain, excited feeling knowing that he was wrong, and she was right.

She hoped he'd get drunk and throw up at the christening. The image of Jase vomiting all over his boss's baby girl made her laugh… until she cried.

As she got close to Viv's, she couldn't help but feel sorry for herself. Other than her two daughters, there was nothing she loved in her home. Jason's demands on her were exhausting. She sensed that it would all come to a head someday, and, when it did, she would be the loser. There was nothing she could do to stop it.

Then she closed her eyes just for a second or two to clear her head and calm down. She took a deep breath and shifted her thoughts to the day ahead.

Riley couldn't wait to see here longtime friend. She knew there wouldn't be a lack of things for them to talk about while on the beach. First, of course, would be Viv's two months touring France. Then, she expected they'd discuss their respective husbands. She hoped they might find time to talk about special things happening at her salon, too.

She told herself, *"This is going to be a perfect day. It's going to be something special. I can feel it."*

6

The Breeze

The day was already sunny and warm.

It was just before 10:00 when Riley pulled into the circular driveway at Viv's house on Summit Avenue. Viv sprang from her house and waved wildly at Riley's arrival.

Riley turned off the engine and jumped out of her car. With big, bright smiles, they hugged and squeezed each other while spinning in the driveway.

"I've missed you, Viv. Two months in France looks good on you!"

Viv was a beautiful friend to Riley. They had gone to grammar school together, had the same first boyfriend, sang together in the school play, and were the Maid of Honor at each other's wedding.

Viv was always there for Riley. They trusted each other explicitly to never divulge any of the secrets they shared. Riley envied Viv's beauty, even though they were equals in this all-important category. Riley loved the way Viv made her laugh. She was always telling Viv that she couldn't live without her. Early in their life together, Viv had confessed to Riley that she loved her.

"Riley my love, I've missed you, too."

Viv pulled away so she could get a good look at her, "I'd say you've dropped two sizes since I was away."

"Yeah, you're right about that. Have a really, good look," as Riley spun around to show her friend her tiny butt.

Viv changed the subject, "Okay. Enough about your cute, little ass. Which you know I love to squeeze. I need to hear all the latest crap that you've not wanted to share with me in your wonderful emails."

Riley lost her smile and said, "You're right about that. There's much crap to discuss. But, first, let's get to the beach."

Ten minutes later, they turned off Western Avenue onto Persons Beach Road. Just after they crossed the bridge over the Mousam River, they pulled into the first space. They were pleased to see that they beat everyone else to the beach.

After they stepped out of the car, Riley went to the back and opened the hatch door. She pulled out a picnic basket, two beach chairs, a blanket, towels, and a beach umbrella.

Reaching for the umbrella and the chairs, Viv smiled at her friend and proclaimed, "I'll take care of these. That picnic basket is yours. It looks heavy."

"Not really. Just something to eat and two bottles of Chardonnay."

"Uh oh. I think someone wants to gain back those two sizes today."

Viv struggled with the umbrella before starting down the path to the beach. The ladies laughed along the way as Viv kept dropping her cargo.

The sand was hot, but they'd travelled the path so many times before that they both knew to keep their flip-flops on until they found their favorite spot on the beach. As usual, it was to the right about fifty feet away, far from the rocks. It was low tide. The beach seemed to stretch to the horizon.

They'd loved the beach from the very first time their mothers had brought them as little girls. The sand was clean and smooth. The Sandpipers picked and scurried along the water's edge, racing to escape the shallow waves that slid ashore. Seagrass was everywhere at the back of the beach and swayed in the gentle offshore breeze. Altogether, this beach was like a fantasy come true. It was a Mecca for two wonderful friends who shared the enjoyment of a very special life together near the sea.

They reached their destination. Riley dropped her picnic basket first then Viv dropped her load. They laughed again as they both descended onto the sand.

Riley whined a little out of breath, "Why do we always drag all this shit to the beach?"

Viv agreed, "Wouldn't you think? We're old enough to know better. I suggest next time, we just come naked."

"I like that idea. Let's do it. Do you think Parsons Beach would survive if we came here naked?"

"Nah. Who gives a shit? Just put me in the ground!"

Riley had a good laugh at her friend's suggestion. She'd missed the way Viv occasionally took song lyrics and spun them into her crazy expressions.

The heat of the sand worked its way through their beach clothes. Viv jumped up complaining, grabbed the blanket, and threw it down. They both jumped on.

"The beach on the French Riviera was never this hot."

With sudden sadness in her eyes, Riley told her friend, "I wouldn't know. I've never been. I don't expect to go there, either."

Pulling her sunglasses down over the bridge of her nose, Viv turned to her, "Uh oh. I thought this was going to be all laughs today?"

"When we talk about traveling, I can't help but think about the times Jase and I've had over the years trying to make our vacations work for us. You know how his mother always goes with us and the kids."

"Weren't you going to ask Jase to stop taking Caryn with you every time you go away?"

"Yeah, I tried. But, he just got mad at me for even suggesting there was a problem."

"So, nothing's changed between you two?"

"I've been trying to make this marriage work, Viv, but it's very hard. Jase doesn't think he's doing anything wrong. And, his efforts to control me are getting worse."

"You told me once that your sister thought you should have divorced him a long time ago."

"Yup. But, she seems to have forgotten she ever said that to me. She's on his side now, totally. It really bothers the shit out of me."

"I never thought you should have married Jase. He didn't treat you well even back when you were teenagers."

"My friend, I didn't know any better back then. I thought I was in love with him. But, I was wrong."

Riley moved closer to Viv, "You know my troubles with Jase started with his mother. Damn her! She's hated me from day one."

"That asshole. I've never liked him or his mother, either. He's no good for you."

Trying to put on a smile, Riley changed the subject, "Let's talk about something else. Shall we?"

"Of course, I'm sorry to dredge that all up."

"No. I brought it up, not you. Tell me about France."

Viv's face lit up, "Wow. There's so much to tell. Where to begin?"

As she began to tell her stories about France, Riley caught sight of a beautiful white sailboat not far off the beach with its sails full of the warm, morning air. She noticed the Arundel Yacht Club pennant flying from the top of the mast. She remembered that Owen had told her the other day that he docked his boat at that yacht club.

"*Hmmm? I wonder...*," she thought, as a soothing breeze crossed the beach on its way out to sea.

A small whirlwind of dust spun past.

Riley kept looking at the man at the helm. She struggled to see who it might be, but she couldn't make him out. It appeared that he was looking at the beach. She smiled and waved to the anonymous sailor. He smiled and waved back. She shuddered as a chill ran through her body. She watched the man and his boat sail on until it was out of sight.

At the same time, *Airship* passed an all but empty Parsons Beach, Owen noticed on his starboard beam a lone beach umbrella with people in its shade. They appeared to be two women out enjoying another beautiful Maine morning.

One of the women kept her eyes on Owen. Oddly, she smiled and waved at him. He smiled and waved back at her.

For a moment, he thought, *"Is it possible? No. Not a chance. That would be too much of a coincidence."*

He decided to put his thoughts of Riley aside and get back to the job of sailing to Perkins Cove. He couldn't help it, though, and looked back one more time at the umbrella on the beach and the vision he wished was beneath it.

Riley pointed to the sailboat passing not far offshore, "Isn't that a beautiful sight? You know, after all these years, we've never gone sailing? Not once."

Viv reacted to her comment, "Nah. Not for me. I'd be throwing up all over my shoes. Hey, you know me. I'm gonna do the things that I wanna do."

"Ha! But, if you were with some hot guy, he'd be romancing you and you wouldn't get sick at all. It could get pretty exciting out there. Think about it. You'd be rockin' the boat..."

Viv shook her head, "Hey! What's goin' on here? You horny or something?"

"Yeah. I guess I am. Sorry."

Riley looked back at the sailboat one last time and squinted to get a better look at her skipper. But, she still couldn't tell if it was him.

So, she turned her attention back to Viv, and the two women spent the next three hours sitting in their beach chairs under the umbrella drinking wine and talking about Viv's tour of France and, of course, Monaco.

They laughed at Viv's husband's inability to either speak or understand any part of the French language. The two of them enjoyed the many mistakes Frank made all across France.

Viv concluded, "It's really true what they say about the French. They hate everyone, including themselves."

Riley nearly choked on her Chardonnay, "So, is it safe to assume that you're happy to be home?"

"You've got that right. France is a beautiful, romantic country with lots of history, charm, and grace. And, the food over there is so incredibly good. But, we love Maine and missed it very much."

Riley responded to Viv's comment, "We missed you, too, Viv. By the way, you must be tired of eating all that great gourmet food over there.

You want a baloney sandwich?"

7

The Cove

Owen's voyage went better than planned.

At 11:10, *Airship* reached the outer marker at the entrance to Perkins Cove on its original and only tack. As the red navigation buoy passed amidships on the starboard side, the Nav' system's timer read fifty-five minutes. He took note that he beat his best time by just over two minutes.

He eased the helm into the wind to luff the main and the jib then turned on the engine. Once the sails were furled, he eased the throttle 'Forward' and headed in toward the Cove.

He loved entering Perkins Cove. This was classic New England. Maine at its best. Up and to the right, lobster buoys hung from the backs of the shops. To the left was the residential side with its beautiful homes and charming cottages.

A high, wooden footbridge over the entrance to the cove linked the two sides.

Airship's mast was so tall that the two sections of the narrow draw in the middle of the bridge needed to be opened, making room for her mast to pass through.

Owen set *Airship*'s engine to 'Stop' then grabbed the docking lines and fenders from below. When he finished tying them off, he jumped back into the cockpit to regain the helm.

He grabbed his air horn and let go with one short blast 'asking' anyone on the bridge to push the red lift button to open the draw. Once raised, he eased the throttle 'Forward.'

As he'd done so many times before, he cautiously maneuvered the mast through the open space on the bridge above.

Once inside, the bridge draw was closed behind him.

He maneuvered *Airship* slowly around the boats that were at anchor everywhere in the crowded cove. He passed the floating dock on his starboard side then brought *Airship* one hundred and eighty degrees about before he carefully edged her port side up to the dock.

A couple of local teens on the boat dock offered to grab the lines from Owen to tie her off.

As the boys pulled *Airship* close to the dock, her rubber fenders squeezed tighter making that eerie, gnawing sound boaters knew so well. She moved gently closer then stopped.

The teens secured the lines on the docking cleats and waved to Owen.

He waved back, "Thanks, guys. That was great!"

He turned off the engine and went below to make his arrival call to the Coast Guard. The instruments were shut down and the circuit breakers turned off. He went back up to the cockpit, closed the cabin door, and set the lock.

Just as he put his boat keys in his pocket, he heard a familiar voice coming from the parking lot a few steps above the dock, "Ahoy, *Airship!*"

Bill Stafford walked down the wooden dock ramp, “Hey, Skipper. How ya' doin'?"

Owen stepped through *Airship's* port boarding gate, "You know all too well how I'm doing. I'm captain of this beautiful boat and happy to see my best friend."

They didn't hesitate to shake each other's hand and attempt a hug.

Perkins Cove was always busy. But, it was busiest on any summer Saturday. Yes, it was a tourist Mecca, but Owen liked the feeling he got moving among the crowd. It was always a fun place to be, and it took his mind off home.

The two walked across the parking lot and dodged one of the tourist-packed Ogunquit Trolleys. A small girl sitting with her mother at one of the open trolley windows smiled and waved '*Hello*' to Bill. He gave her a wink and waved back.

Owen said, "Hi" and "Good morning" to most everyone they passed.

They entered the Oarweed Restaurant just before 11:30, as planned.

The hostess, greeted them, "Good morning, gentlemen. Would you prefer to eat outside or inside today?"

Owen answered for them, "On a day like today, Alice, you know there's no other place to be but outside."

She smiled at them, "Knowing you, Mr. Flynn, I didn't need to ask. Did I?"

"Nope. Thanks, Alice."

She walked the two of them through the dining room and out the back door. As usual, the restaurant was packed. But, luckily, an outside table had just opened up. It was right next to the entrance to the Marginal Way. They both enjoyed people-watching, so their table location was perfect.

It was not close to noon yet, and the Marginal Way was already packed.

Alice told them, "Jeff will be your waiter. He'll be with you shortly. Be patient, we're very busy today."

Owen responded, "No problem, Alice. We're not in any hurry. Thanks."

He turned to his friend, "It's good to see you, Bill. How're the kids?"

"They're just terrific. Bill junior scored a hat trick last Friday in his soccer match against Wells. It was raining, and I wish they'd postponed the game until it stopped. But, you know those soccer coaches."

"I'm sorry I missed the game. Let me know when he plays next, and I'll be there to cheer him on."

After lunch, Owen paid the tab, and both men pushed their chairs back from the table. They stood and walked through the opening that brought them onto the Marginal Way. They joined the crowd strolling up the hill around the cove.

Bill was quiet for a few steps then asked, "So, what's up, Owen? You seemed eager to have lunch with me today."

"Yeah. You're right. You know the Boon Island Race is coming up, and I need..."

Bill finished his sentence for him, "... someone to run your foredeck for you?"

"Yeah. How'd you guess?"

Bill laughed, "I figured you were going to bring that up. You know I'm the only man alive who can do the job for you. Of course, I'll do it!"

They shook hands, "Thanks, Bill. I was hoping you'd volunteer. With you up front along with the rest of the regular crew, I just know we're going to win this one."

"You bet. We made a couple of mistakes last year and snuck in second. Ain't gonna do that again, are we?"

"Nope. Not at all. I'll call the crew and let them know we're in."

They reached the top of the first hill and paused to look out at the ocean beyond the cove. A nearby bench became empty so they took a seat to continue their conversation.

"I found a new barber last week."

Bill thought it an odd piece of news to bring up, but he went along anyway.

"They did a good job. A little too short in the back, but that'll get fixed in time."

"Damn! You sound just like Julie."

Bill saw sadness in his friend's face, "How're you two doing these days, buddy?"

Owen hesitated a bit, finding the question hard to answer. They'd always been honest and open with each other, and there was nothing they couldn't talk about.

"That's a tough one, Bill. I don't know. Julie and I've been together for thirty-eight years, and the love we once had has left us. That's assuming we were ever really in love, at all."

Bill leaned closer to him, "I've never told you this, but I didn't think you two were good for each other at all. You and Julie are two very different people."

"Things are getting worse between us, Bill. We don't seem to have any laughter left. And, I realized years back that we lacked real affection for each other. We stopped being intimate long ago."

"I'm sorry, Owen. I really am. Despite your problems, you two are very good people. You both deserve the best. Where do you think this is headed?"

Owen turned his gaze to the shallow waves below them, "I need to work harder at our relationship. We've both invested a lot in this marriage. We've got three wonderful kids and three adorable grandchildren. If there is any real love there, somewhere, it's worth the effort to make things better."

"Look. You've been a good husband to her. Everything's going to work out for the best. But, you know that I'm always here for you whenever you need me. No matter what might happen to you two. Right?"

Owen placed his hand on Bill's forearm and agreed, "Yes. I do my friend. Thanks."

After another hour of talking and walking along Marginal Way, the two men got back to the dock and said their good-byes.

Owen boarded *Airship*, got underway, and started back to Kennebunkport.

Along the way, his thoughts turned to Riley. He was confused and concerned. His marriage was no longer working. A sense of shame passed over him. There was no easy solution to it.

But, Riley's face kept jumping in front of him. He knew it was wrong. He felt guilty, again, if only for a moment. He had to stop thinking about her. But, no matter what he thought or said to himself, it didn't change anything.

So, he just smiled at her image and sailed on home.

8

The Encounter

A week went by and Owen went into Kennebunkport to pick up supplies.

The day was perfect with a cloudless, blue sky. A cool, gentle breeze off the water promised a perfect day ahead.

He parked behind Alisson's, walked across Western Avenue, and headed for Standard Marine in Austin's Alley. As he crossed the street, Riley was leaving Compliments Gallery in Dock Square. His heart skipped several beats before he found his smile.

She smiled broadly at him, "Hey! Good morning, Owen!"

At first, he couldn't speak. She was dressed in pure white culottes and a multicolored top that was open at the neck. The morning sun lit up her blonde hair. Her dangling earrings perfectly matched the colors in her top.

He settled down and found his words, "Hi, Riley. You're looking lovely today. Just taking a break from the salon?"

"No, just doing some shopping in town then heading up to Portland. It looks like Crystal did a good job with your hair, huh? Shorter hair makes you look younger. And... even more handsome."

The moment turned awkward.

He thought to himself, *"What do I say now?"*

Not letting the moment pass, he told her, "Well, in all reality, Crystal made me look better than I deserve."

"Now, that's not true at all. I can tell you're a man who deserves everything he gets. I saw that Crystal setup another appointment for you next week. I'll look forward to seeing you then."

As she started to turn, she said to him, "Take extra good care of yourself. We need to see you back safe and sound."

Then she stopped. A thought went through her head, and, before she moved on, she asked, "By the way, I was out on Parson's Beach last week with a friend, and I saw a sailboat go by. For some reason, I thought it might be you."

Owen's eyes lit up, "Maybe it was. I was out last week sailing to Perkins Cove. I did see two ladies under an umbrella around ten thirty or so. I didn't see anyone else on the beach that morning. Do you think that was you?"

Riley reached out with her hand and gently touched his upper arm, "I'm pretty sure it was. We were the only ones there. I hoped it might be you, so I waved."

"Then, it had to be you. I waved back. How 'bout that?"

"I guess it was fate and some good timing that we were looking right at each other at the exact same moment. Next time, you'll have to stop and pick me up. I'd love to go sailing with you."

He fumbled a bit then made certain that his invitation didn't scare her off, "Okay. Good. How about your friend. Would she like to join us?"

She squeezed his arm, "Probably not. She gets seasick pretty easy."

"Well, if there's anybody else you'd like to have join us, feel free to invite them along. We'll have a lot of fun. Especially if it's a day like today."

"It will be. I promise."

Riley continued to stare at Owen as she extended her hand to shake his, "It's funny how we keep running into each other like this. Out on the ocean or here on land. You never know where or when it might happen next."

"Yeah. You're right."

Owen felt guilty, again. He knew he shouldn't spend time with Riley, on land or at sea. But, he couldn't help it. He liked being with her, And, he liked it a lot. He wanted it to continue, to go on. He tried shrugging off what he knew was wrong. But, nothing worked.

"It was really nice bumping into you, today, Owen. I look forward to seeing you at the salon again. Have a really good day today, okay?"

"Yes. I will. And, I'm glad we ran into each other, too, Riley. Stay safe, huh?"

She smiled then continued on her way.

His first thought as they parted was, *"Oh my God! What is this? I'm excited to see her. I shouldn't be! I can't be! This is just wrong."*

He watched her cross Western Avenue. When she was safely on the other side of the street, she stopped and looked back at him. She waved. He gave her a quick wave back and smiled.

He thought to himself, *"Sailing alone with her could be a problem."*

She was happy she saw Owen. She was surprised at the way he looked at her when he was in the salon.

She wondered, *"Why did he smile at me so much? It seemed that every time I looked up, he was watching me. I'm not sure, yet, if it's a good idea to go sailing alone with him."*

Late that afternoon, Riley returned to Kennebunkport from her shopping in Portland. Driving home, she felt decidedly different. She was happy. And, it was the first time in a very long time that she'd felt so good.

After putting her car away in the garage, she found Jase sitting in the dining room. His work papers were spread out, completely hiding the table.

"Hi, Jase," she said quietly as she passed him with her bags.

"Where the fuck have you been? You've been gone all day!"

"I've been shopping in Portland."

"Why didn't you call me to let me know where you were?"

She spun around to face him, "Why do we go through this every time I go out? I'm a big girl. I'd like to think that, as an adult, I could go out without you always confronting me!"

He pushed his chair back, popped up, and pointed at the window, "Don't you know? There are lots of men out there who would give their left testicle to spend just half an hour alone with you."

"What do you think I'm doing? Do you think I'm a hooker, off to find lonely men who want to have sex with me?"

"Of course not, but I just don't trust you. Jesus, Riley, my brother Donny called me to tell me he saw you talking with some man at Dock Square this morning. Who was that?"

Riley hated Jase's two brothers and their families. They all lived together in three houses built in a row right next to one another. Jase's house was the middle one, and Riley had no privacy at all. Any in-law, or their children, was allowed to just walk into her kitchen without so much as a knock at the door. She had always felt his family was watching her every move then reporting back to Jase.

"He's just one of Crystal's new clients. I stopped to say hello and to ask if we did a good job for him."

Jase spit his words at her, "So, how many men do you have a special relationship with?"

She knew it was futile to argue with him. He was convinced that she was flirting with every man on the street.

Disgusted, she just turned away from him and started for the bedroom.

She was halfway up the stairs when he continued his rant, "I told you I don't want men in your salon. I want you to turn them away."

"What? You want me to put a sign on the door that reads, *'NO MEN ALLOWED'*? That's just absurd."

Her happy feelings disappeared. In tears, and shaking, she climbed the rest of the stairs to the bedroom and slammed the door.

Jase's suspicions that his wife was flirting with other men had intensified to the point where he couldn't think about anything else. He believed that his wife was doing something, and he was determined to find out what it was.

For privacy, he quietly went out of the kitchen door and called Riley's sister from his cell phone.

Ella's husband, Gary, answered, "Hello?"

"Hi, Gary. It's Jase. How ya' doin'?"

"Awful. Just awful. I spent thirty minutes on the treadmill just now and…"

With his typical display of disinterest, Jase interrupted Gary, "I need to talk with Ella. Is she there?"

Gary knew full well Jase's lack of sincerity, so he simply responded, "Yup. I'll go get her."

In less than ten seconds, Ella took the phone from her husband, "Hey dude, what's up?"

"Well, everything's pretty much okay. But, I think I have a problem. I need a little advice, right now."

"You've come to the right place, love. What's the problem?"

"Well, I'm not really sure. You know how much your sister flirts with other men..."

"Hey... Whoa... Jase, we've talked about this before. Riley doesn't flirt with other men. She's just a good person, friendly to everyone. She's nice to both men and women."

"You know I disagree with you and have for years. She's always looking and smiling at men wherever we go. She tries to dress provocatively. Fortunately, I've managed to stop it from going anywhere every time she's tried it."

"You're going too far, Jase. Yes, Riley's beautiful. But, that doesn't mean that she's trying to hit on every man she meets. She has a handsome husband, two wonderful daughters, a beautiful home, and... a really, really, terrific sister. Why would she ever want to risk losing all that? I've told you before, I know Riley better than anyone. Yes, we have a really crazy family, but Riley and I are the only normal ones. She comes into the salon and keeps to herself. She just does her job and goes home. You're making her out to be someone she's not. If anything, she's just very quiet."

"Okay, I understand. I'm just so worried that someday she'll have an affair with some asshole, and I won't know about it until it's too late to stop it."

"I know. I know. But, Riley's completely faithful to you. You know you can count on me, babe. I really believe it. And, I want to prove it to you. If you want, I'll keep an eye out at the salon and see how she behaves when men come in for haircuts. If I have time, I'll watch to see where she goes."

"You mean follow her?"

"I wasn't thinking that. Do you want me to?"

"No. She'll just recognize your car. Plus, I don't want her to get pissed off at you."

Ella ended the call whispering to Jase, "Okay. But don't worry. I really want to help you, darling. You know you can always count on me to protect you. I'll let you know if anything's going on that you need to know about. I promise, love."

"Thanks, Ella. You're the best. This is a perfect family, and I can't have anyone mess it up for me."

9

The Question

Owen returned for his next haircut.

He parked his car and headed for the salon. He hoped to see Riley again, but he knew he needed to keep his feelings in check.

When he rounded the corner onto Western Avenue, Riley was sitting on the bench outside the salon. She smiled at him.

He stopped at her feet, "Good afternoon, Riley. How've you been?"

Leaning toward him on her elbows, "Okay. Just a bit tired. It's been a long day."

He sat next to her on the bench, "At least now you can go home and get some rest."

"Not really. My last client will be here in fifteen minutes. I thought I'd sit out here and catch a breath of fresh air. Salons get filled with lots of really stinky stuff floating in the air."

He started to get off the bench, "Yeah, I noticed. Anyway, please excuse me, I don't want to be late for my appointment."

She placed her hand on his arm to keep him seated, "Crystal's running a little late. You really don't want to wait inside. Trust me."

Sitting back down, he agreed, "Okay. I'll wait out here. I need some fresh air, anyway."

He moved closer to her. Her eyes were still sparkling.

The sun was lighting up his green eyes, too. She couldn't help but stare at them.

She moved her hand from the back of the bench to his shoulder, "I was thinking about our seeing each other when you sailed passed us at Parsons Beach. That was bizarre."

He agreed, "We couldn't have timed it better if we'd tried. I like the idea of being at the same place you are."

She had an idea for a clever response, but decided to change the subject back to sailing, "You know? I've spent all my life watching sailboats from the beach, wondering what it must be like to be out there sailing. It's got to be more than just fun. I'll bet it's exciting, too."

"Exciting, it is! It's the closest thing I know to flying. You're in control of everything except the elements. You need good wind, and you have to adjust the controls all the time. I really enjoy the feeling I get when I climb aboard my *Airship*!"

He tapped her knee and continued, "If I'm not mistaken, I think you invited yourself to go sailing with me not long ago."

"Oh? Did I do that? I'm so sorry. That was dumb of me."

"Please. Don't worry about it. We'll see. Maybe someday I'll actually get you out on my boat."

"Yes, I'd like that. By the way, why do you call it *Airship*?"

"Well, I've spent a lot of time flying, first with helicopters then with passenger jets. So, it didn't take me long to come up with the name."

"Why do you refer to your boat as 'her'?"

"Well, it's a tradition that goes back hundreds of years. And, I don't have the authority to change the rules."

She nodded her acceptance of his answer then changed the subject again, "Crystal told me you grew up around here. Did you go to Kennebunk High?"

"No, I went to Phillips Exeter."

"Ha. So, you're a preppy... I like that."

"Really? Most people think preppies are assholes."

She laughed and patted his knee, "We're all assholes, Owen."

The door to the salon opened, and Crystal poked her head out, "Hey, you two. What's going on out here? It's time to get back to work."

Riley and Owen got up off the bench and headed for the salon. He opened the door for her.

"Why, thank you, sir. I didn't think there were any men left who knew how to treat a lady."

"Well, my mother was half Irish and half Italian. She taught me a lot about life, but mostly she taught me how to treat a woman. What's more, I know that she's watching me every minute. So, I can't screw it up."

Riley paused at the door, "You know, you're really something special. I like your mother. And, I think I like you, Mr. Flynn."

"I like you, too, Mrs. Reed."

After they entered the salon, Riley headed for her manicure desk.

Owen sat in Crystal's chair, "It's good to see you again, Owen. Anybody tell you that you have a really nice smile?"

"Well, thanks, Crystal. I don't know exactly what people see of me. At my age, I'm happy just to have all my teeth, never mind a nice smile."

"And, beautiful teeth they are. You're very lucky indeed. So, what are we doing today?"

He turned slightly trying to see the back of his head in the mirror, "Let's thin it out a lot more this time and leave it a little longer in the back."

She snapped the stylist cape around his neck then looked at him in the mirror, "Got it. How about if I let you see the back with my hand mirror. You can tell me what you think. I can always take it off, but... Well, I'm sure you know that old barber's saying."

"Yeah. I've heard it a lot over the years."

Crystal was impressed with how quickly Owen and Riley got along. She didn't spend time thinking about it. She just felt good that Riley was happy and smiling so much with Owen in her salon.

So, she bent down and whispered in Owen's ear, "I just love working for Riley. She's a smart and fun-loving boss. We get along so well together. I think you get along well with her, too."

He whispered back, "Yeah. I like her. She's a smart lady, as you say. And, she's also very attractive."

Crystal spent the next twenty minutes cutting, trimming, and thinning Owen's hair. Twice she showed him the back of his head with her hand mirror and both times he asked her to take a little more off.

Finally, she reached the point where he was satisfied, "There. That's it."

"Okay. Now, let's get over to the sink so I can wash it out."

After rinsing his hair, they returned to her station where she clipped a few loose ends. She brushed his hair and ran her fingers through it. Finally, she turned on her hair dryer to blow the clippings away.

When finished, she unsnapped the cape and pulled it off, "There you go, Owen How'd we do?"

"Crystal, thank you. You've done a nice job, again, for me. I like it. By the way, you have to promise me that if you and your husband ever decide to move to Florida, you'll let me know in time for me to move down there so I can keep my appointments with you."

"That's a deal."

He paid her with a five-dollar tip. She thanked him with a big hug. They scheduled his next appointment.

As he was about to leave, Crystal whispered to him, "I thought you should know. The other day, Riley checked my calendar to see when you were coming in today. Then she called her client over there and asked her to move her manicure back half an hour. I think she was outside on the bench waiting for you today."

Owen's eyebrows went up, "Oh, really? That's interesting... Thanks."

Suddenly, he had an inspiration. Instead of heading for the door, he walked back to Riley's manicure desk.

He apologized to Riley's client for interrupting her then knelt down at the side of the desk. He slid both of his hands on top of the desk with his fingers spread out.

Riley wondered what it was all about. She stopped polishing her client's nails and looked down at Owen.

He smiled up at her, "I have a very important question to ask you."

She snickered, "Okay. How can I help you?"

He hesitated for about two seconds then asked, "Do you think I need a manicure?"

Riley thought for a moment then laughed, "Mr. Flynn, everyone needs a manicure. Just let me know when."

Riley arrived home just after 7:00 that night. She parked her car in the garage and went into the house.

Jason couldn't wait to confront her, "Where the fuck have you been?"

"Christ, Jase. You know I've been busting my ass all day at the salon."

"Apparently, you were not in the salon all day. You spent some time with another so-called client of yours sitting on that bench outside the salon."

"Fuck you, Jase. What? Your family's spying on me again? I was just taking a break and getting some fresh air when Crystal's client showed up for his haircut. We just talked for a few minutes then went inside."

Screaming, he couldn't hold back, "I didn't hear it from my family. Your sister called me and told me all about it. According to her, you spent half an hour with him laughing and joking around. She told me that he then ended up kneeling down and talking with you at your desk."

She was quietly outraged and thought for a second, "*Ella? What the Hell is she doing?*"

He continued to scream at her, "You're showing way too much interest in other men. And, Ella tells me this one's an old man. She told me he's in his sixties, for God sake. What the Hell is wrong with you?"

"Right. He's an old man. So, it's absurd to think that I'd be interested in him at all."

"You bitch! Do you think I'm that stupid? Flirting with other men has suddenly become spending time with them. Where will this lead to next? What's this asshole's name?"

"Look, Jase, he's not important. His name's not important, either. Just let it go."

Unable to control his anger, Jason lunged at Riley, and pushed her up against the kitchen wall.

With both hands pressed hard against her, he yelled, "Goddamn you, Riley. You're going to tell me his name. Now!"

More frightened of Jase than she'd ever been before, she had to answer, "Owen."

"Owen who?"

"Why do you want to know his name?"

"You know I'll find out anyway."

She knew he'd get it from Ella, "Flynn. Owen Flynn."

"I warn you, Riley. Don't ever have this guy, Flynn, in your salon again. And, if you're having an affair with this dickhead,

I'll kill the both of you!"

10

The Manicure

Two days later, Owen left his office an hour early.

He needed to spend time at the salon before going home. When he left for work that day, he didn't tell Julie he was getting a manicure after work. He just didn't think he could provide her with a convincing enough reason for him to get one.

After parking his car, he rounded the corner and headed for the salon. Riley was waiting for him, again, on the bench.

She was anxious to see him. She didn't really know why. All she knew was that he was a special man. A mysterious man. She wanted to know more about him, but she worried that she'd like what she heard.

She replaced her deep thoughts with a bright, open smile, "Hey, Owen. It's really good to see you. I was worried you might not show up today."

He sat next to her on the bench, "You need to get to know me better, Riley. I'm never late for anything, and I let people know if I can't make an appointment."

"I wish there were more people like you in this world. I have too many clients who just don't give a damn about being on time. And, some of them just blow me off and don't show up at all."

"Well, I'm here... and on time. So, let's get it over with. By the way, this is going to be the first manicure I've ever had."

"Hell, then! This is going to be fun."

She stood up, took hold of his hand, and tugged him through the salon door. They both laughed at her eagerness to get him in the chair at her manicure desk.

They passed the stylists and their clients. Most of them smiled when Riley comically pulled Owen to his appointment.

She announced to everyone, "I was just told that this guy has never had a manicure in his life."

Most every lady in the salon cheered for him.

Riley was having a lot of fun. She was happy to have Owen as her new client. When he looked at her, she felt good about herself. She felt instantly younger with no cares at all. It was a feeling she hadn't had for far too many years.

He sat in the chair in front of her desk. There was a vintage desk lamp to her right, and her tools were neatly organized and laid out in front of her. On the wall behind her were two hundred or more bottles of nail polish neatly arranged along nine rows of a metal display rack.

He looked up at the colorful polishes, "I'm not getting any of those, am I?"

"Of course, you are! It's part of the whole manicure package. Before I finish, I'll find a color that matches your eyes."

"So, you're joking. Right?"

"Maybe. Maybe not. I've done a lot of manicures for men, but only one of them asked for polish. I painted his nails with 'Pink Blossom.' He was an interesting guy to say the least. He's never been back."

While she cut her client's hair, Ella pretended she didn't hear the discussion between Owen and her sister. She mentally began to put together her report to Jase that she would deliver to him that night.

Riley tapped the towel spread out on her desk and instructed Owen, "Ready? Put both hands on the towel, please, sir."

"Yes, Ma'am."

He placed both hands on the towel. She started with his right hand, took her file, then shortened and smoothed the edges of all five fingernails. She trimmed the cuticles and cleared out anything that might have hidden under his nails.

He couldn't stop looking into her eyes. Nor, could he help what happened next.

He leaned forward and whispered to her, "You are the most beautiful woman I've ever met."

Riley paused at the comment. She looked at him without her smile. There was suddenly a seriousness that forced her to respond. She spent seconds trying to find the right words but failed.

"I'll bet you say that to all your manicurists."

He smiled, "Yeah. How'd ya' guess?"

Riley attempted to continue the manicure, but her head was spinning. It took several seconds before she found herself, again.

She couldn't gather the words to return to their conversation. Instead, in silence, she completed her work on his right hand then repeated the steps of the process on his left.

She opened a jar of Sugar Scrub, scooped out a few fingers-full, and started to rub his right hand. She took her time massaging both sides of his hand at the same time, moving over his wrist and up his forearm.

Ella interrupted, "Riley calls that a hand-job."

He smiled up at her but said nothing. Riley just rolled her eyes, embarrassed at her sister's clumsy joke.

She repeated the Sugar Scrub massage on his left hand.

There was no further comment from Ella.

Riley broke their silence, "Okay. Let's go wash this stuff off, shall we?"

She entered the breakroom first and turned on the faucet. Once happy with the temperature, she asked Owen to rinse off both of his hands and arms to clear the Scrub away.

He rubbed his hands together, "My hands have never felt so smooth. That's amazing stuff!"

She helped him dry off with a towel. When done, she took hold of both his hands and rubbed her thumbs across the softness.

While staring into Owen's eyes she said, "Every man should have hands this soft. It would make a woman very happy."

Out of sight and alone, the two stood facing each other, holding hands in silence.

"Jase, it's Ella. I think something's going on with Riley. Remember I told you about this guy, Flynn? Well, he came in today and..."

"Flynn? Owen Flynn? I told her he was never to be in her salon again. Why in Hell did he come in this time?"

"Well, this time she gave him a manicure."

"Shit! Why the fuck does he need a manicure? This is getting out of control, Ella."

"Jase, be careful with this. I don't see or hear anything to worry about..."

He interrupted again, "Damn it. I told her I don't want men in her salon at all for anything. That includes manicures, haircuts, nose jobs, nothing!"

Her plan was working, "Jase. You've got to let go of this. Nothing's happening. It was just a manicure. And, you cannot attack Riley when she gets home tonight, either. If you do, I'll be blamed for it. I promise you, if that happens you'll never hear another word from me again about Flynn or any man who comes in the salon. I'm doing this as a favor to you. I love you, and I want the two of you to be happy."

"Happy? Oh yeah, I'm happy all right. Don't you know how this'll look if she's having an affair? I'll never hear the end of it from my mother."

Ella took a deep breath, "I know, Jase. I know. Just keep in mind to stay cool. If anything, ever really does happen, you know you can count on me."

"Yes, I'll do my best. We just have to keep this away from my mother."

Then she lied to him, "You know I'll take good care of you and Riley. Don't worry."

11

The Coffees

Owen had spent a lot of time thinking about Riley.

He couldn't get her out of his head. But, he wasn't really trying to, either. He enjoyed the special feeling she gave him, and he needed to see her again.

At 5:00 the next morning, he took a shower while Julie slept and got dressed. He quietly descended to the kitchen, gulped two cups of coffee then headed out the door to his car.

He drove into town and parked in his usual spot behind Alisson's. He walked to the local coffee shop and bought two medium coffees with a handful of cream cups and little bags of sweetener. Then he headed to Riley's salon with the coffees in a cardboard tray.

Riley had just opened the salon and was sweeping the floor when Owen tapped on the window. She looked up and was excited to see him. She put her broom away and went to the door.

She opened it halfway and stuck her head out, "Deliveries are around back, please."

Laughing, she closed the door.

He opened it and poked his head inside, "Hey! It's me. I didn't know the rules. Sorry. But, if I have to go all the way around back, this coffee's going to get cold."

"You're right. We can't let that happen. Come on in, then."

He stepped through the entrance and followed her to the breakroom. He put the coffees on the counter and moved up onto one of the two stools. She climbed onto the other one.

"What brings you in today? And, so early?"

"Well, I couldn't sleep anymore so I got out of bed at 5:00. I was thinking you might be here early, as well. I guessed right."

"That you did. And, thanks for the coffee. I didn't have time to make any this morning so this is really nice of you."

She removed the lid of her coffee cup and poured in a container of cream and one bag of sweetener. She stirred the mixture and tasted it to be sure it was perfect.

"By the way, my sister will be in around 7:45. I don't trust her. It would be better if you weren't here when she comes in. Okay?"

He nodded and looked at the clock over the door, "Got it."

He turned to Riley, "So, what's going on in your world? Outside the salon, that is."

"You don't want to know."

"Yes, I do. I see you're wearing a ring so I assume you have a husband. Any kids?"

"Yes, Lauren fourteen and Kelly sixteen. They're typical teenage girls. Their hormones are bubbling, and they both have boyfriends, neither of whom I like. Kelly has always had difficulty with me. I don't know why. She's been a real pain in the ass from the day she was born. Lauren, on the other hand, has been my best friend forever."

"That's too bad about Kelly. I found that teenagers can be a big problem no matter what we do. But, you survived."

"I'm not so sure about that. Only time will tell. How about you? Any kids?"

"Well, let me see. If I remember right, I have three children. My daughter, Colleen's thirty-seven. My oldest son, Evan, is thirty-four. And, my youngest son, Sean, is thirty-one. They're all good kids. At least that's what I taught them to be. I could have been a better father for them. I was tough at times, but I was fair, too. I hope they know how to be good parents. I also have three grandchildren."

"I bet you're a good granddad. Do you spend a lot of time with them?"

"I really don't get to see them much. Their all spread out all around the country now."

He returned to his questions, "So, what else should I know about you, this beautiful lady in front of me?"

"You mean stuff like my height, weight, and blood type?"

"That's a start. But, I bet there's more."

Riley looked at the ceiling for things to tell him, "Let's see... I grew up in Wells then moved to Kennebunkport when I married Jason. Everyone calls him Jase."

"How long have you been married to Jase?"

"Nineteen years."

"And, how old were you when you guys got married?"

"Okay. Let's see. I was eighteen when Jase and I got married. Then, Kelly was born three years later."

"So, that would make you thirty-seven. Am I right?"

"Yeah. You're correct. So, you have a daughter my age?"

"I guess I do. That would make me old enough to be your father."

"Is that a problem?"

"Why do you ask?"

"No reason. Just curious."

She wanted to learn more about him, "So, how about you? You're married for how long?"

“I married Julie, my sister's best friend, when I was young. We’ve been married for a long time."

"So, would you say that Julie is the one you'd been looking for all your life?"

"Nope."

After another twenty minutes, Owen left the salon and drove home with his untouched coffee.

Julie was waiting for him in the kitchen, "So, what have you been up to this morning?"

"I just went for some coffee and came home."

She stood up to challenge him, "Coffee? You had coffee before you left. The coffee maker is still on."

He couldn't find an answer to her question so he made one up, "I couldn't sleep anymore and got up at 5:00. I was bored so I just went for a ride. That's all."

"And, you just picked up some coffee before you came back home?"

"That's right."

Julie didn't believe him and grabbed the paper cup from him. It was still full, but cold.

"You son of a bitch! What's going on? None of what you just told me makes any sense. You bought coffee just before coming home, and it's cold?"

"Look, I picked up the coffee when I went on my ride. Okay?"

"And you didn't drink any of it? You're lying to me. Why?"

He fumbled around, eager for an explanation, "Sweetheart, I stopped in town to talk with some people I know. There's nothing to get upset about."

"Bullshit! You're up to no good, and I'll find out eventually. I just know it."

She raced out of the kitchen. He didn't go after her. Instead, he just sat at the table and held his head in his hands,

"Shit. That was really dumb."

12

The Call

A few days later, Owen returned for another haircut.

He was excited to see Riley again, but he knew he had to be careful. He didn't want the attention he was paying her to become an issue with the stylists, especially with Riley's sister.

Crystal was ready for him, "Hey, Owen. Right on time, as usual!"

He sat in her chair and looked up at her, "Hi, Crystal. How're you doin'?"

"Busy. Very busy. You'd think after 5:00 people would want to be home having supper. But, no..., they want to get their hair done."

"I'm sorry about that, Crystal. I don't get out of the office until 5:00 or 5:30, and..."

"Oh, no. I'm not talking about you. You're easy. It's the ladies I have to deal with."

She opened the cape, snapped it behind his neck, and went to work, "So, you seem a bit unhappy today. What's got you down?"

"One of my crew almost drowned in the Boon Island Race the other day. He's lucky to be alive. I still can't get over it."

Crystal stopped and moved around to look him in the face, "Oh, my God! What happened?"

"It's a long story, so I won't go into the details. Bill Stafford, one of my crew, was hit by a really strong wind gust that sent him overboard. And, he wasn't wearing his life jacket. We had to go back but couldn't find him. Fortunately, another boat was there to help him."

Crystal's mouth went wide open, "That must've been terrifying! Is he okay?"

"Yeah, he was scared there for a while. He's okay now, though. But, we were pretty sure we'd lost him. Oddly enough, the name of the boat that pulled him out of the ocean was *My Hero*. He was really lucky that they got to him in time."

Riley walked over to Owen, crossed her arms, and leaned back against Crystal's counter, "So, Mr. Flynn, how'd you like your manicure?"

Crystal interrupted her boss, "Owen just told me that one of the crew on his boat went overboard and got eaten by a shark."

"What?!"

Owen laughed and corrected Crystal, "Don't mind her, Riley. She's just joking around, as usual."

He then answered Riley's question, "I liked the manicure very much. Actually, it was incredible. But, I'm probably not going to recommend it to my friends."

"Why not?"

"No, it's not a bad thing. It's about being in touch with one's feminine self. I think some of my friends are stuck in their manhood."

"Well, I hope you are a regular client of mine."

He bent toward Riley and whispered, "I hope so, too. I think next time, though, we shouldn't make my nails shine. My wife saw it immediately and asked what had happened to my fingernails. I had to make something up."

"Oops! Sorry…"

Riley attempted a smile then returned to her manicure desk. Crystal finished Owen's hair.

Before she removed the cape, Crystal whispered to him, "She's been talking to me a lot about you. She asked me questions I don't know the answers to."

Owen whispered back, "I'll see what I can do."

She continued, "Just be careful around Ella. I don't trust her at all."

"Thanks, Crystal. I will."

Before he got out of the chair, Riley walked past him and out the door.

He made his next appointment with Crystal and paid her with his usual tip. He said goodbye and left the salon.

As he turned the corner to enter the parking lot, Riley was standing against the wall in the alley.

"Hey, Riley. What's up?"

"I'm just waiting for you. I'm really sorry about the shiny nails. Won't do that again. Promise."

"Thanks."

She continued, "I have a question for you. I thought we should stay out here where it's a bit more private."

He turned and leaned next to her against the wall, "Okay. Ask away."

"Why did you stop into the salon the other morning? It was awfully early."

"Yes, it was. But, I couldn't sleep and needed some coffee."

"But, you told me that you already had two cups before coming in. What's the real reason?"

He was quiet for a moment, "Okay. The truth is you kept me up all night."

"You were concerned about me?"

"No, not at all. Just the opposite. You seem to be occupying a large part of my brain lately."

She moved closer to him against the wall and slid her right hand onto his arm, "I know what you mean. I can't get much sleep lately either."

Out of the blue, he sprung his question, "Would you like to have lunch with me?"

"Oh my... I didn't expect that."

"I'm sorry. I guess I threw that at you too quickly."

"Look, Owen, I'm flattered by your invitation," she said then lied to him, "but I must tell you that I'm a happily married woman and just can't accept."

Embarrassed, Owen attempted to recover, "Oh, Riley, I'm sorry if I crossed the line just now. I didn't mean to. Please, forget that I asked."

"Oh no. Don't be concerned. It was very nice of you to ask."

"How about this? I'll give you my work number. If you ever change your mind, just call me. Okay?"

"All right. But, that doesn't mean I'll call."

"I understand. It's just in case you change your mind."

He took an envelope from his jacket pocket, ripped off a blank corner then wrote down his office phone number in Portland. To be discreet, he didn't write his name on the paper.

She took it, put it in her pocket, and looked long into his eyes. Neither said a word. Nor did they move. They just stood facing each other. For a moment, it was a little awkward.

After what seemed an eternity, she squeezed his hand, "I'm okay. Really. Don't worry. I'll see you when you're back at the salon again. Take good care of yourself and try to stay away from sharks for a while, will ya'?"

"Yeah, I'll try. Bye."

"Bye."

She turned to go back to the salon while Owen headed for his car. As she got to the corner, she stopped and looked back. Owen stopped, too, and turned to look back at her. They both smiled and waved goodbye.

As he headed back toward his car, his smile disappeared. Hers did, too.

Owen thought, *"My head is going to explode. I'm confused. Is Riley flirting with me? Am I flirting with her? This is all going so fast. My heart is taking over my brain, and I can't stop it. I don't want to stop it!"*

Early the next day, Owen was in his office at the airport.

He couldn't sleep again, but for a different reason.

"I blew it yesterday. How stupid am I? We're both married, and we shouldn't be doing this."

He attended two meetings in the morning then went to lunch with one of his managers. They discussed several problems with flight operations and agreed to put together a plan to quickly resolve them.

On the way back to his office, he was interrupted by thoughts of Riley, *"What's wrong with me? I just can't get her out of my head. She's amazing!"*

He returned to his desk and sat back. While looking out the window at one of United's 737s climbing off the runway, the phone rang.

"Hello, this is Owen Flynn."

"Hi."

He recognized her voice and sat up in his chair, "Riley?"

"Yeah' it's me... I'm shaking like crazy..."

"Why?"

"Because I shouldn't be doing this. But, I can't help it. I want to go to lunch with you."

He began to shake a bit as well, "This is crazy, but I want to see you, too. Very much. How about tomorrow, 12:30? I know a really good restaurant on the harbor in Portland."

"Okay. 12:30's good with me. Where should I meet you?"

"How about here at the airport. It's off the beaten path. Would it be okay if you pick me up here?"

"That's fine. I just don't know where to go."

He gave her directions to the United check-in door.

She continued, "I apologize if I sound nervous about this. I am! Very..."

"Riley, it's just lunch and nothing else. I think we need to spend time just talking about things like life, work, families, and... us."

"All right, let's do it. But, just this one time. Agreed?"

"Agreed."

13

The Complication

The next day, Riley drove to the Portland International Jetport.

She followed Owen's directions then called him from her cell phone, "I'm here. I'm on McKay Avenue at the United door."

"Okay. Great! Give me three minutes. I have to take the elevator to the first level."

"Hurry. There's a cop walking toward me. I think he wants me to move."

Owen smiled, "That'll be Sergeant Belmont. If he gives you a hard time just tell him you're here to pick up Owen Flynn. I'll be right there."

As she predicted, Sergeant Belmont tapped on her driver-side window.

She opened it, "Are you Sergeant Belmont?"

"Yes, Ma'am. Thank you. You'll need to move out of the way. If you're waiting for someone you can park your car in short-term parking."

"I'm just waiting for Owen Flynn. He told me to tell you he'd be right down. He's in the elevator right now."

Belmont straightened up, "Not a problem, Ma'am. We all like Mr. Flynn. He's a good man. I'll keep the traffic out of the way for ya'. You have a good afternoon, now."

He stepped behind her car and began to direct traffic around her.

Owen emerged through the automatic glass doors.

As soon as she saw him, she realized he didn't know her car, so she jumped out and waved to him, "Over here!"

He saw her, waved, and walked to her car.

Before getting in, he waved at Sergeant Belmont, "Thanks, Jimmy."

"Not a problem, Mr. Flynn. Have a good afternoon."

Owen slid onto the front passenger seat, "Hi, there. So... what brings you to Portland Airport?"

"You! I'm starving! Let's go eat a cow or something."

Owen directed her out of the airport onto Westbrook Street then over the bridge to downtown Portland. They turned off Commercial Street onto Commercial Wharf and parked in DiMillo's lot.

She looked at the restaurant in front of them, "I've always wanted to eat at DiMillo's. But, I don't get to eat out that much."

"Well, let's go see if it's worth the trip."

They walked through the entrance and were greeted by the hostess at the front desk, "Good afternoon, Mr. Flynn. Welcome back. How are you doing today?"

"We're doing just fine, MaryAnn. Thanks."

MaryAnn couldn't help but look at the beautiful, young woman accompanying Owen, "Welcome to DiMillo's On The Water, Miss."

"Thanks very much. I'm happy to be here."

MaryAnn looked back to Owen, "I'll have Robert show you to your table, the one with that view of the harbor you like so much."

He handed her a ten-dollar tip, "Thanks, again, MaryAnn. You know how to take good care of me, and I really appreciate it."

"You're always very welcome, Sir. And, thank you! Enjoy your day!"

MaryAnn handed Robert two menus as he welcomed them, "Good afternoon, Mr. Flynn."

He then pointed Riley toward the stairway, "Please follow me, Miss."

The three walked through the paneled lower deck, and up the stairway to the sunlit upper deck. Their table had a spectacular view of Portland Harbor. It was a beautiful cloudless day with boats of all shapes and sizes motoring or sailing past them.

Owen pulled out a chair for Riley and slid the seat under her as she sat.

"Why, thank you, sir!"

He moved around to his chair, "You're very welcome. I like the view here a lot. Boats everywhere."

She looked out at the harbor with dozens of boats moving in all directions, "How do they all keep from crashing into each other?"

"Nothing's ever perfect. There are some accidents every now and then, but you rarely see one of them sink."

After they laughed at his joke, he changed the subject, "I'm glad you changed your mind about lunch today. I'll bet it wasn't an easy decision."

"That's for sure. My husband doesn't trust me and is always accusing me of cheating on him."

"Well, having lunch with me is not cheating on your husband. It's just lunch."

"That's not the way Jase sees it at all. If I so much as look at another man walking down the street, he'd be screaming at me for flirting with him."

"Okay. Let's agree that, from now on, if I'm walking down the street, you're not going to look at me."

"Now that would be impossible."

They took time to look over the menu then ordered a simple, seafood lunch. They each asked for a glass of wine.

An hour went by as they ate, drank, and learned more about each other. She told him about her struggles in the early days of her salon. He heard about her sister complaining, whining, and gossiping while styling her customers' hair.

Then, she described how Jase and she met during high school. She disclosed more about him and how he had become a big problem for her. She told him about his need to control her moves, her thoughts, and even her words. She explained that Jase learned how to control people from his mother.

Owen listened carefully, focused on her every word, "I guess it's safe to say that life's not been easy for you."

"No, not at all. But, the best part of my life right now are my two daughters."

"I'm glad there's some goodness in your life."

"Well, not really. Lauren has Cystic Fibrosis. It's been very difficult for her and for me. When we first found out that she had CF, it was devastating. We knew absolutely nothing about the disease and spent a lot of time learning about it and understanding it. It was especially important to focus our energy on the care we needed to give her."

She looked down for a bit then up into his eyes, "She needs me so much!"

He rested his hand on her arm, "Riley, I'm so sorry for you and for your family. It's got to be really demanding, taking care of Lauren while raising another teenage daughter. And, having to deal with a difficult husband."

"Some days I feel like I can't go on. I'm not a religious person, so I don't kneel down and pray. I just get up and do what has to be done."

"Does your husband help with Lauren, I hope?"

"Are you kidding? He says his job around the house is just bringing in the money, and it's my job to take care of everything else. It's kind of like the caveman days at my house. He's the hunter, and I'm the gatherer."

"You're a tough lady, Riley. I wish I could help you."

"Good. Besides the laundry, can you walk the dog every four hours, make all three meals for us, vacuum the house, wash the windows, and change the sheets on our beds every week? And, that's just for starters. We'll see how you do before we decide to keep you."

"Okay. I'll start tomorrow morning at 5:00."

She reacted, "Good. Now, can we change the subject?"

"Of course. What do you want to talk about?"

"You."

"Me? Okay. I'm really not that interesting, but fire away."

Riley sat forward in her chair and moved her elbows onto the table.

She put her chin in her hands and looked closely into his eyes, "So, are you happy at home?"

"Ha... That's a Hell of a question."

"Yeah, I know. So, what's the answer?"

He grinned at her and was speechless for a while, "No."

"That's it? No? You're not happy at home?"

He placed his elbows on the table just opposite hers. He put his fingers together then rested his chin on his folded hands.

"Not long ago, you asked me if I'd found the woman I'd been looking for all my life."

"As I recall, you said 'Nope.'"

His eyes went sad, "Maybe I've been looking too hard."

A bit embarrassed, he continued, "I'm sorry. I really don't mean to get you involved in my personal life. My view is that no one's perfect. If we want to be truly happy, we just have to find a way to accept each other's flaws. To make adjustments."

"But, sometimes there's no way around it. Sometimes the problems are so deep they can't just be fixed."

"I know what you mean. It's difficult. Very difficult, sometimes."

"I don't mean to pry, but just how would you describe the woman of your dreams?"

"So, you're not going to let me off the hook. Are you?"

"Nope."

"Okay. The woman of my dreams is much more than just smart and attractive. She's understanding, thoughtful, accepting, kind, funny, sweet, a bit audacious, affectionate, and wildly intimate."

Riley sat back in her chair and laughed, "Do you need more time to think about it?"

"No, I don't need more time. I guess I've been thinking a lot about it lately."

"So, have you ever met anyone who even came close to that description?"

He looked down for a couple of seconds then back up at Riley, "Yeah. Actually, I think I have. Any chance I can call you sometime?"

"Hum... I'm not so sure that would be a good idea."

She stopped and thought for a moment before she added, "We'd have to be very careful."

She studied his eyes then continued, "But, it would be nice."

With a few more questions answered in her head, she agreed, "Yeah. Okay. I'll give you my number."

Joking, he asked her, "Do you need more time to think about it?"

Taking hold of her purse, she found a pen and a piece of paper and wrote down her phone number. She passed it to him then moved her hand onto his.

She leaned forward and whispered to him, "This is going to get complicated."

"Yup... I think it already has."

14

The Mistake

A few days later, Owen got the nerve to call Riley.

He'd hidden the piece of paper with her phone number in his desk at the airport. He'd been there for the morning and finally made the call.

The phone rang four times before it was picked up, "Hello?"

"Hi, Riley?"

"No. This is Kelly. My Mom's not here. Who's this?"

Owen was shocked to learn that, by mistake, the number she gave him was her house phone, not her cell phone.

He tried to recover, "Oh, I'm sorry, Kelly. I'm Owen, one of your mother's clients. Is she there?"

"No. Can I take a message?"

"Okay, thanks. Please let her know that I can't make the appointment next week, and we need to reschedule."

While writing a note for her mother, Kelly asked, "Who'd you say you are?"

"Owen. That's Owen Flynn."

"Thanks, Mr. Flynn. I'll let her know. What is your number?"

He then made the same mistake and gave Kelly his cell phone number, "Thanks, Kelly. Have a good day."

After they ended the call, Owen shouted into his work phone, "Fuck!"

Kelly ran to her father in the garage, "Daddy. Some guy just called looking for Mom."

Jase stuck his head out from under the hood of his car, "Oh? Who was it?"

She looked at her note, "His name is Owen Flynn. He said he's a client of Mom's and had to change his appointment."

Jase wiped his hands on a rag and took the note from his daughter, "Thanks, Honey. I'll give this to Mom. Okay?"

"Okay, Dad."

As Kelly went back into the house, Jase's thoughts turned to his wife, *"That little piece of shit is going to pay for this!"*

He pulled out his cell phone and called Riley at the salon.

Betsy, one of the stylists, answered the phone, "Good morning. Looking Glass Salon."

"Hi, Betsy. It's Jase. Is Riley available?"

"Hi, Jase. Let me ask her."

A few seconds later, Riley picked up the phone, "Hi. What's up?"

"You piece of shit! Your boyfriend just called the house, and Kelly answered the phone."

"Wait a second, Jase. I need to go out back."

She excused herself from her client and went out the back door.

She got on the phone again and asked, "Whoa... Who called me at the house?"

"Flynn. Owen Flynn. He said he needed to change his appointment with you. I knew something was going on between you two..."

"That's ridiculous. There's nothing going on. He just needs to change his appointment? What's wrong with that?"

Jase spit his words into the phone, "Well, let's start with his being your client. How many times do I have to tell you that you're not going to have men as clients? Second, why did he call the house instead of the salon?"

Riley struck back, "First off, Jase, I have plenty of men who come in here to get a manicure or a pedicure from me. It's part of my business. And, they do so before or after one of my stylists cuts their hair. This is how a salon works."

"This is not how my wife's salon is supposed to work!"

She became even more agitated, "I'm not going to change my services just to satisfy you. It brings in more clients, it helps them, and I bring home more money which should make you very happy."

"We don't need your money. You know that I make enough for both of us. You should just sell the damn place."

Riley fought back, "I've been running this salon successfully for many years. I'm not going to hang it up now just to make you happy. Jase, you need to trust me. He's just a client of mine. Crystal cuts his hair. That's it. He's like sixty-five years old or something."

"Trust you? You've got some guy calling our house looking for you? Why in the Hell did he call the house?"

Shaking her head, "I have no idea. I'll just call him and find out."

"No. You're not going to call him. I have his phone number right here. I'll call him for you."

"Jase, you can't..."

He hung up on her.

15

The Threats

Riley stayed out the back door of the salon and called Owen on his cell phone.

He answered, "Hello?"

She was shaking, "It's Riley. My husband's about to call you. Kelly told him that you called the house. Be careful. Call me at the salon and let me know what he says to you!"

She hung up immediately.

A second after Owen hung up, his phone rang again, "Hello?"

With an angry, high-pitched voice, Jase yelled into his phone, "Is this Owen Flynn?"

Pretending he didn't know, he asked, "Yes, it is. Who's this?"

Jase raised his voice even higher, "This is Jason Reed. What the fuck are you doing calling my house looking for my wife? Huh, asshole?"

Owen stayed calm, "Hey, wait a minute. I apologize, Jason. I had to change an appointment with her and got the number from 411. I thought it was her salon."

"No way, man. You're lying to me. My sister-in-law works at the salon, and she told me that you're not just one of Riley's clients. It's much more than that. Isn't that true, buddy?"

"Jason, I have no idea why your sister-in-law told you that, but it's not true. Believe me."

"I don't believe you, and I don't believe Riley. You better not show up at the salon ever again. You understand me? If you do, I'm coming after you, and you're not going to like what happens."

Jase hung up on him.

Owen called Riley back.

She answered immediately, "You okay? What happened?"

"Well, he's pissed off all right. I really screwed up, Riley. I'm sorry."

"Don't be. I gave you the wrong number. A simple mistake. A big one, but simple. I'd say you got a good look at my problem."

"Well, he threatened me and told me not to go to your salon any more. Also, you need to be really careful. Your sister is feeding your husband all kinds of crap about us."

"I know, Owen. Ella's really screwed up. She's always been jealous of me. I know her too well. She'd like nothing better than to make me look bad just so she can look good."

"Listen. I'm not worried about Jason or Ella. We can manage them. We just need to be careful. I need to stay away from the salon and let things cool down."

"You mean let things cool down between us?"

"Not at all, Riley. Anything we do just needs to be kept very secret. We have to assume that Jason's family, and yours, are watching us."

"You sure we can keep this a secret?"

"Yes, I'm certain of it. Look, my wife's going to be with her sister in Boston shopping all day tomorrow. Can we meet somewhere just to talk a bit? That's all."

Riley thought for a moment, "Tomorrow? I don't know, Owen."

He countered, "I think, given the problem we're facing with Jason, we need to figure out what we should do about it. It shouldn't take long."

"Jase is going to his mother's summer cottage up at Old Orchard Beach and won't be home till after 6:00. I think we could be safe somewhere. It just has to be away from town."

"How about up in Biddeford?"

"Where in Biddeford?"

"How about the Biddeford Shopping Center? It's between the Turnpike and Route One."

"Yeah. I know the place. I've only been there once. Where can we meet?"

"There's a Planet Fitness on the left side as you drive in. Let's meet behind it. Okay? How about 2:00? Everything's going to be all right. I promise."

She felt better, "Okay. I need a break from all this. And, I really need to be with you."

They said their goodbyes and hung up.

On her way back to her desk, Riley stopped at Ella's station, "We need to talk."

Ella was between clients, sitting in her stylist chair, playing solitaire on her noisy cell phone.

Riley demanded, "Let's go."

She then turned around and headed to the back door while Ella rolled her eyes and slowly got up. She had a disgusted look on her face as she dropped her cell phone into her purse and followed Riley to the back of the salon. The two went outside and closed the door behind them.

Riley started in, "What the Hell are you doing? You've been telling Jase bullshit about me, and I'm disgusted with it."

"What are you talking about? I haven't said anything to Jase. It's none of my business what you do or don't do."

"You're damn right it's none of your business. What's happened to you? You told me once that you thought I should have divorced Jase long ago. Now, all of a sudden, you're on his side?"

Ella yelled at her sister, "I'm not on anyone's side. I'm just trying to make a living at my damn job. So, get out of my way."

With a finger in Ella's face, Riley screamed, "You better stop this and leave me alone. Or else."

"Or else what? You can't threaten me."

"This is not a threat. It's a fact. If you don't stay out of my personal life, I'll tell everyone what you don't want them to hear about you and Jase. That's Mom, your husband, my girls, the whole fucking town if necessary."

Ella pushed Riley out of her way, "Oh? Try me, bitch!"

16

The Kiss

With Julie off to Boston and Jase at Old Orchard Beach, the coast was clear.

Owen arrived at the shopping center before Riley. He pulled into the parking lot then around to the back. There were plenty of open spaces, and he selected one farthest away from any windows or doors. A dumpster provided even more privacy.

He had worried that Riley might not show up. Their relationship had been an open one because they hadn't really done anything wrong.

But, that was about to change.

Ten minutes passed before Riley pulled in next to him. She looked at him through her side window with half a smile. She turned off the engine, got out, and closed the door behind her. She turned around and found that Owen had already gotten out of his car and come around to open his passenger door for her.

He gave her something that appeared to be a smile, "Hi."

"Hi."

The air was filled with dread.

Owen spoke first, "About yesterday. Like I said, I'm so sorry. I really fucked up."

"No, it didn't go well at all. Jase was all over me about you. He demanded that I drop you as a client."

"I don't blame him. I'd do the same thing if I were him."

"And, my fucking sister told Jase that you and I were having an affair."

"Shit!"

"What do you think we should do?"

"I could still come in for haircuts. We just need to keep it secret."

"No. I can't trust Ella to keep her mouth shut. She'll be watching and reporting everything to Jase."

Owen sat back and looked up for a moment, "Then, as long as I don't go to the salon, it won't be a problem. I'll just have to find somewhere else to get my hair cut. That'll be easy."

"As much as I hate to say so, you're right. I'll let Crystal know."

Neither of them said another word. They both turned to the front and stared through the windshield at the blank, gray wall of the Planet Fitness in front of them.

Then, without looking at her, he asked, "So, have you ever done this before?"

"You mean hide out next to a dumpster behind Planet Fitness with a man old enough to be my father?"

"Yeah... That's about right... So, have you?"

"Never!"

"Me, neither."

"I'm scared, Owen. I've been married nearly twenty years and have two wonderful daughters. If Jase ever finds out that I've spent time hiding out with you, my family will be devastated. No, make that destroyed. And, he'll come after both of us."

"I understand, Riley. I don't know if, or where, this is going. I just believe we can manage to keep whatever happens away from our families."

"I've never cheated on Jase."

"I'm not suggesting that we cheat on anybody. We can end this at any time. We won't hurt anyone."

She was silent for several seconds, "But, that would hurt me."

He took hold of her hand, "It would hurt me, too, Riley. But, maybe we should just stop this now before it becomes more than it is. We can say our goodbyes and go home to our families."

She looked out her side window then back at him, "No. If we did that, I'd be leaving my heart behind. There's something special going on here. A whole lot of planets and stars are lining up just right for us. I can't sleep. All I think about is you."

Owen agreed, "I know. I know. I can't stop thinking about you either. So, let's stop worrying. We'll find a way to make this work. For now, we need to change the subject to something more positive."

She thought for a bit then asked, "Okay. New topic. I'm falling for you, and I really don't know much about you. Who are you?"

"Ah, that's a tough question. Actually, I'm a serial killer and look for gorgeous women to attack everywhere I go."

"I'm pretty sure you're joking. Right?"

"Sure. I got out of the serial killing business years ago. Much too messy. Seriously, though, I'll be sixty-two in a couple of months. And, yes, that's probably your father's age. I flew helicopters in Vietnam, and when I retired from the Army, I became a commercial pilot for United Airlines. I flew lots of miles until I landed at my desk as Director of Operations for United up in Portland. I love sailing, dogs, and, as I think I told you, my kids. Not necessarily in that order. In my spare time, I write books. Oh, I almost forgot... and, I still can't get over the fact that I'm not eighteen anymore."

Riley had been listening closely to every word while watching the sparkle in his eyes. Before her was an exciting human being, like no one she'd ever met. He was a man who knew how to treat a woman with respect and kindness, who listened more and talked less, who survived a war, and flown thousands of people safely all over the planet.

"Tell me about the war."

"Okay, but I'm going to make is as short as I can. So, here goes. After college, I joined the Army. They made me a helicopter pilot and sent me to Vietnam for the first time in 1969..."

"Jesus. I wasn't even born yet."

"Yeah. I figured that. Anyway, I won't get into the gory stuff. All I'm..."

"That's just fine with me."

He continued, "All I'm going to say is that I believed in our mission over there. The South Vietnamese were under constant threat from the Communists in the north. They asked for our help, and we sent a lot of people over there. Unfortunately, the war went on too long. The politicians made sure of that. But, over fifty-eight thousand Americans died there. The television news back home wasn't good. For the first time, people watched a war live from their living rooms. But, the worst part was the unrest on college campuses. A lot of students protested the war. I think they just didn't want to get drafted and sent there to die."

"And, drafted means?"

Owen smiled at her, "Oh, that's right. You wouldn't know about the draft. The government just up and told a lot of young men that they had to join the Army or go to prison. It was a bad time in our country. Eventually, our president back then just declared 'peace with honor' and ordered everyone to come home. We were gone, but the war raged on for the Vietnamese. After we left Vietnam, it took only two years for the Communists to finally take over. A lot of good people died over there for nothing."

"My God that's terrible! You said you flew helicopters?"

"Yes, I did. But, I told you I wouldn't talk about the gory stuff. I'll just tell you that for the two years I was there I was shot down twice. I was only injured, but some of the guys who were with me didn't make it back alive."

She was humbled and thought, "*Wow. How do I follow that?*"

He continued, "That's pretty much it in a nutshell. How about you? Who are you, Riley Reed?"

She was a bit embarrassed to answer, "I don't come close to that in any way at all. I'm very impressed. And, I have to say you don't look sixty-two at all. More like eighty-five..."

She laughed while he tried to figure out if she really believed he looked eighty-five. He decided she was just joking and laughed along with her.

She went on, "I'm just a thirty-seven-year-old mother of two girls, both of whom I love dearly. I told you about my daughter, Lauren, and how she has Cystic Fibrosis. We have a poodle named Roger that we love dearly. I didn't go to college, but instead I started my own business when I was just nineteen. I've been pretty good at it so far. And, I've been married to the same asshole for just about twenty years."

"When did you figure out that your husband was an asshole?"

"The day he confessed to me that he asked my sister for phone sex."

Owen's eyes went wide open, "What the Hell? You have to be joking."

"Nope. He really did it. And, it was just after Jase and I were married, too."

Owen couldn't believe what he'd just heard, "So, Jase isn't just an asshole. He's an idiot, too."

"Right. I made a really bad decision to marry this creep."

"Does anyone else know about this?"

"Just my sister, Jase, and me. And, I told her yesterday to stop blabbing about you and me, or I'd tell the world what the two of them did."

"Are you telling me that she actually did it? I mean, he asked her for phone sex just after you were married, and she did it with him?"

"Yup. I know it's unbelievable. But, Jase actually told me they did it."

Shaking his head, "That confirms it. He's a very stupid man. "

Riley just shook her head in agreement.

Owen continued, “So, what other crazy things do I need to know about you?"

"Nothing. I don't have anything important to tell you. I'm a very dull person. Besides, I'd rather just spend our time together talking about us."

"Okay. I'd like that, too. By the way, you forgot one thing about yourself."

"Oh? What did I miss?"

"Only that you're the most beautiful woman on the planet."

Riley back-handed his shoulder and laughed, "That's not true at all."

"It certainly is true. I've flown thousands of women all over the world, and you're clearly the most beautiful woman I've ever met. And, you're not allowed to argue that with me. Understand?"

"Yes, sir. But, I'll remain quietly under protest."

"Thank you."

Raising an issue, she added, "Anyway, my husband wouldn't agree with you."

"Really? Then he's a bigger fool than I thought."

"And, he keeps telling my family, and me, that I'm as dumb as a doorknob."

Owen bowed his head then looked up at her, "Riley, in the short time that I've known you, I find you to be very smart. Listen, you've been quite successful in your business. And, profitable, too. That's more than ninety-nine percent of other small businesses. Only smart people do that!"

"I think you're a little biased about that aren't you, Mr. Flynn?"

"Maybe. Maybe not. I can tell you that I've worked with some pretty dumb PhDs in my career. And, so far, you're smarter than any of them."

They fell silent.

Suddenly they found themselves looking at each other with just the hint of a smile. But, soon it became an intense look, filled with something that had been growing inside of them ever since they first met. They hadn't let go of each other's hands. There was excitement, and a hint of lust, in their touch.

Smiles slowly returned to their lips.

They needed this moment. They needed this sharing. They knew what was coming and unwilling to stop it.

Owen drew closer to her. She moved closer to him. He bent forward. They studied each other's eyes. Their lips pulled closer. With eyes still open, they kissed. At first, it was a simple, shallow kiss. Then it quickly became a lingering and persistent kiss.

At first, it tested their readiness. There was a bit of hesitation, followed by a hint of acceptance. It became a kiss filled with excitement and, yet, a danger they'd never known. But, it was real and it was beautiful.

He stopped and fell back. He looked into her eyes, and asked, "Hey. You wanna' read a good book?"

With surprise across her face, "You mean, right now?"

They laughed at his suggestion.

"No, silly. Not now. I thought of you when I bought it. It's really a good story called *'Nights in Rodanthe'* by Nicholas Sparks. I think you'd like it. I did."

He turned around, took the book off the back seat, and handed it to her.

"What's it about?"

"Well, it's a really good love story about two middle-aged people who each try to deal with their own, personal struggles, but find love together at a vacant inn on a Carolina beach."

"I really love stories like that. I want to read it. Can I ask how it ends?"

"Nope."

"Well, damn. That's not nice."

"No one should disclose the ending of any book, or movie, to anyone. What's the point? Why would you ever want to read it or see it? What if you'd never seen *'Sixth Sense,'* and I told you how it ended?"

"I've never seen *'Sixth Sense.'* How does it end?"

He laughed at her, "You're crazy."

They stopped laughing and went back to kissing, which continued for close to an hour.

When they stopped, she said, "I think it's time to leave."

"What?"

"I mean, if we keep this up, it's going to go somewhere I'm not yet ready to go."

"Yeah, I know what you mean. But, we're quite far away from that, yet. If at all."

"I like you a lot. No, make that a whole lot. I'm ready, and I'm not ready. I have a lot to discuss with myself right now."

"I understand. This is happening very fast. We need more time to consider where we're going with this."

He stopped for a moment then suggested, "No, never mind that. How about, instead, we just stay here for a little while longer and see what happens?"

She pushed him up against the car door, laughing, "You're disgusting."

"Yeah. Come to think of it, I guess I am."

She opened the book, scanned a few pages, and discovered several passages underlined in red.

"You underlined some of the words and sentences?"

"Yeah. Sparks has written about things that made me think of us. Also, take a good look at page 143."

She flipped to page 143. In addition to several underlined sentences and phrases, he had circled the page number.

"I don't understand. What's the significance of the page number?"

He told her, "Well, I was thinking we need to be able to communicate with each other without people knowing what we're saying. It's what I'm going to call a 'love code.' Each digit represents the number of letters in each word."

With a slight frown on her face, she asked, "So, what does '1-4-3' stand for?"

"Someday I'll tell you, but not just yet. Unless you can figure it out for yourself."

"This'll drive me crazy. Are there any 'love codes' that I really need to know?" she asked.

"Yes, there are. Lots of 'em. Maybe you'll figure them all out, or maybe you won't. I know you'll come up with some yourself."

He added, "Like you said... It's time to go."

She scowled back at him, "I know. But, I want to stay longer."

"Riley, I'm worried that Jase or Julie might be looking for us."

She checked her phone, "Shit! I turned my cell phone off to keep it quiet, and Jase called me three times."

She listened to her messages. He last called her over two hours earlier.

Owen checked his phone. No messages at all.

"What the fuck am I going to say to my husband? He knows he can reach me any time, night or day. I just know he's going to come after me when I get home."

"Hey, tell him you went shopping and the phone battery died. It happens to people all the time."

"Yeah. Okay. I'll try. I just need to get home right now, though."

They spent a couple more minutes hugging and kissing. He got out of the car and walked around to open her door. They wrapped their arms tight around each other. They kissed again.

Riley smiled, "143, huh? I think I know what it stands for."

He put his finger up to her lips, "Don't say a word. I want you to come up with three love codes before we see each other again."

"When will that be?"

"How about in an hour?"

"I wish..."

"Me, too. Think about when we can get together again. Can I call you at the salon?"

"Of course. Just be careful. My sister might answer the phone."

"Okay. What days is she not there?"

"Tuesdays and Thursdays."

"I'll call you on Tuesday, then. Okay?"

"Yeah. That works. The salon is pretty much empty during lunch hour. Call me around noon or 12:30."

They held each other's hand for a moment before she got into her car. She opened her car window and smiled at him. He bent down and kissed her goodbye.

Riley started her car then backed out. As she pulled away, she beeped her horn and waved.

Owen waved back and began to worry.

It was just after noon on Tuesday. Owen called the salon.

Riley answered, "Good afternoon. Looking Glass Salon."

"How would you like to go sailing with an old fart?"

When she heard his voice she quickly got up and moved toward the breakroom for a little privacy.

"No. Not at all."

"Huh?"

"I'd much rather go sailing with you."

He laughed, "Good! What day is best for you?"

"This Sunday is supposed to be a beautiful day. And, Jase has got to go back to Old Orchard Beach again. I'll be free all day."

"Sunday, it is then. How about 1:00 at the yacht club?"

"What about your wife?"

"She prefers to stay as far away from my boat as possible. She gets seasick, even at the dock."

"Okay. It's a deal, then. What should I bring? Any special clothes, like Topsiders?"

"Nope. Sneakers and jeans will do just fine. Be sure to wear warm clothes. It can get pretty chilly out there even on a warm day. And, bring a hat and sunglasses, too."

She saluted the phone, "Aye, aye, captain. Avast ye matey. Or something like that. I guess I'll need to bone up on my pirate talk."

"No need. I'm pretty sure we're not going to be attacking any other boats while we're out there."

"Damn! I was hoping for a little high-seas adventure."

"Not this trip. Maybe next time."

"Owen. I can't wait to get out on that boat with you. I need it badly."

"So, do I."

17

The Boat

It was Sunday morning, just after 11:00.

Jase knew his mother hated Riley. He also knew the feeling was mutual. So, he took their two daughters and left the house to go visit his mother.

Riley watched from the window as they drove off to be with 'the bitch.'

Assured they were not coming back any time soon, she went upstairs. She took off her pajamas in the bedroom then went into the bathroom for a quick shower. When she finished, she stepped out of the tub and dried herself off.

She returned to the bedroom. On the far wall was a full-length mirror. She stood naked in front of it. She was pleased with everything she saw.

Having thought about it all night, she put on a sexy, white lace bra and matching panties. It stimulated her to know that Owen wouldn't be aware of the secret that was hiding underneath her yachting clothes.

She jumped in her car and smiled on her way to the yacht club.

Owen had finished his breakfast, listened to the news, and dressed for the day's adventure with Riley. He was more than excited, but he had to be certain not to give away any hint of it to his wife.

Julie descended to the kitchen and avoided greeting him, "What time will you be home?"

He offered a quick joke, "I'm not sure. It depends on how far I go. With such a beautiful day, I'm thinking Ireland would be nice."

Julie didn't react. She wasn't even listening for his answer. She just wanted him out of the house.

"Well, you're on your own. My sister's coming to town, and we're going shopping for the day. You can stay out there as long as you want. I don't give a shit!"

"Why do you dislike our boat so much? There was a time when you enjoyed going out on it, even if we just stayed tied to the dock."

"I never enjoyed it at all! Years ago, I went with you because I thought it made you happy. Now, I don't care at all."

"Oh, yeah. Sorry I asked."

"And, nowadays, I just don't like being alone with you out in the middle of the fucking ocean with you yelling at the seagulls and screaming at me about being a-lee. Whatever the Hell that means."

"It means watch out, I'm tacking. In other words,…"

"Fuck you and that disgusting boat of yours, too."

She spun around and climbed the stairs to the bedroom. The door slammed shut behind her.

Owen's next thought was, *"Okay!... It's time to go sailing."*

Ten minutes later, he pulled into the yacht club parking lot and looked for Riley. She was already there waiting for him. She opened her window and waved to be certain he saw her.

He waved back.

They got out of their cars and met at the entrance to the dock.

They shook hands in case anyone they knew was watching, "Good afternoon, Mrs. Reed. How are you today?"

"I'm doing very well, thank you, and really looking forward to sailing with you, Mr. Flynn. It looks like a perfect day for it. Don't you think?"

He looked at his feet for just a second then up at Riley, "It couldn't be better. I think you're going to enjoy your first sail. It's going to be fun."

They walked down the wooden ramp and onto the dock. *Airship* was waiting at the end with its bow headed outbound.

When they arrived at the boat, he looked down and said, "*Airship*. I'd like to introduce you to my friend, Riley Reed. Riley, please say hello to *Airship*."

She curtsied, "Hello, *Airship*. I'm very happy to meet you. I've heard so much about you."

Owen pointed to the boarding gate, "I'll go ahead of you, Ma'am. Please watch your step."

He went aboard and asked for her bag. She handed it to him. Then he took her hand and steadied her as she stepped from the dock onto *Airship's* deck. He helped her into the cockpit.

She turned and smiled at him, "Thank you, captain. This is one big fucking boat ya' got here."

"You know what they say about the size of a man's boat?"

"No, I don't, actually."

After giving Riley a quick tour of *Airship*, Owen asked, "We'll be getting underway in a few minutes. Did you bring your sunglasses and a hat?"

"Oops. They're downstairs in my bag. I'll go get them."

He got up and headed for the hatchway, "No, you stay up here. I'll go get your things. Besides, I have to turn the circuit breakers on anyway."

He climbed down the ladder and opened her bag resting on the counter. He retrieved her sunglasses and hat. He also found a windbreaker in the bag and pulled it out.

He opened the electrical panel and switched on the circuit breakers. He went into the aft cabin and grabbed two life jackets. He pulled out his hat from the wall cabinet along with his foul weather jacket and sun glasses then went back up the ladder to rejoin Riley in the cockpit.

He handed her a life jacket, "Can I show you how to put this on?"

"Let me give it a try first. It looks pretty easy."

She surprised him and put it on correctly the first time. Owen did his next.

"Okay, there's a pretty strict procedure I follow to ensure our safety getting out of here. I'll tell you what you need to do if and when you need to. Okay?"

She saluted him with a smile, "Roger that, big boy..."

"Hey, there's no laughing on a sailboat. This is serious shit."

Riley laughed as she sat down on the starboard seat.

He got back to work and rigged *Airship* for the day's sail. He set the throttle to 'Neutral' and started the engine.

Riley was very patient as Owen moved around the boat doing his sailor thing.

"Okay, we're just about ready to castoff. I just have to go back on the dock to untie the lines."

Once *Airship* was freed, he jumped from the dock back into the cockpit and adjusted the throttle 'Forward.'

Airship got underway.

After the boat moved away from the dock, there was a bit more challenge ahead. As always, the Kennebunk River was clogged with all kinds of boats, moored or underway. So, *Airship* needed to remain at slow speed.

As they passed other boats, he told her of the long tradition for anyone who was on a boat to wave 'hello' to others as they passed by. It stemmed from the tradition in the Royal Navy of saluting another warship and its crew as they passed each other.

In today's world, it was a boaters' way of saying *'Stay safe. We care about you.'* to people they didn't even know.

So, Riley found herself immersed in the tradition and gave every boat they passed a cheerful, "Hey, there! How ya' doin'? Stay safe!"

Owen loved what he saw. Being together, Riley was happy. She was a woman who longed to laugh but had been confined to sadness. He suddenly knew that it was going to be his job to give her what she hadn't asked for, but dearly needed.

And so, it began.

18

The Cruise

Airship passed between the rock jetties leading to open waters.

Owen continued out for a hundred yards then turned *Airship* into the wind. He slowed the engine to provide just a bit of maneuvering against the wind's influence.

"You ready to sail, young lady?"

"You bet your ass, captain."

"Okay. I have to bring the fenders in first. You take the helm and keep her steady. I'll be right back."

"Hey! Wait a minute. Take the helm? Keep her steady? Are you crazy?"

Laughing, "You'll do just fine."

He stepped out of the cockpit and went on deck to pull in the fenders. Once they were safely stowed below, he returned to the cockpit to take back the helm.

Riley pretended she couldn't loosen her grip on the wheel, "I think my fingernails got embedded into your steering wheel."

"Yeah, I know. It'll stop hurting in a week or two," he smiled as he 'pried open' her hands.

Owen flipped on the mainsail's roller furler and hoisted the main up the mast. He then flipped on the jib furler and unfurled the Genny.

With the two sails in place and luffing in the breeze, he called, "Ready about."

Nothing happened.

He looked down at Riley. Her eyes were closed with her face was pointed at the sun.

Owen shook his head, "Oh, I forgot to tell you that before we make any turns I'll let you know with a 'ready about.' That's when you have to duck. 'Cause when I yell, *'Hard a-lee,'* the boom will swing across the deck and knock you off the boat."

"You mean like into the water? "

"You got that right. So, let's try again. Ready about?"

Riley got off her seat and ducked into the cockpit.

He laughed at her and yelled, "Hard a-lee."

Owen turned the helm full about and maneuvered for a jibe as the air began to flow over the stern. The wind caught the sails, and the lines tightened.

They were finally under sail.

He turned off the engine, and it was suddenly silent. The sails were set, the lines were locked down, and the sea was barely moving. The sails were pulling them along.

It was perfect.

While Owen steered the boat from the helm, Riley moved around and got comfortable on the cockpit cushions.

He looked beyond *Airship* to the horizon and pointed east, "Look way, way out there. That's Ireland. My grandmother was born just to the left a bit. I was twenty-six when she died, but I can still hear her laugh. She was a real Irish lass with a love of life and a happiness rarely seen nowadays. I never heard her raise her voice. Not even once. She was a kind and gentle woman with a whole lot of grace in her eyes and in her heart.

We would go to visit her when she lived in Charlestown, Rhode Island. Her special friend would come to visit her for two weeks nearly every summer.

I can still see the two of them grooming African Violets while they sat together at a big plant stand in the sunny, rear window of the dining room.

All I remember was that my grandmother's friend was a kind and beautiful woman.

Before my grandmother died, she told me who she was, *'Owen, you've seen the movie The Wizard of Oz, right? Remember the Good Witch of the North? That was my friend who would come to visit me. I couldn't tell you who she was until she had passed. Her name was Billie Burke.'*

Wow! I was in the Land of Oz and didn't even know it.

My grandfather, however, was a troubled man. He beat my father badly when my Dad was growing up. Grandpa had survived the first and second world wars only to live in pain for the rest of his life. It wasn't a physical pain, but an emotional one. Today it's called Post Traumatic Stress Disorder, or PTSD. Back then it was called 'shell shock' or 'battle fatigue.'

Anyway, you name it, it's not an easy thing to deal with. Every one of us who's been in combat has some degree of PTSD. We all have to learn to manage it. My grandfather's way of managing it was to beat the shit out of my father whenever his head was back in the war."

"Are you okay. I mean, do you have PTSD?"

"Like I said, all of us who survived combat have it. Some more than others. I'm lucky to only have been moderately affected. And, what I do have, I learned long ago to put out of my head. For me, now, it's gone. It's over.

So, I keep watching the future and for my place in it. I've done a lot of good things, but I'm not finished, yet. I have so much more to do before I leave this wonderful world of ours."

Riley stood and moved next to him at the wheel. She put her arms around his waist, looked deep into his eyes, and said,

"I think I want to go there with you. Your future, I mean."

19

The Message

After another hour of sailing, *Airship* was back under engine power.

The water in the river was smooth, with not the slightest ripple.

Riley was relaxing, sitting back on a cockpit seat. The sun was in her face, and she liked its warmth as they motored back to the dock.

"So, did you enjoy the trip?"

"Yes, I sure did! I never thought anything could be so nice and so scary all at the same time."

"There's an old saying that goes something like this, *'If you think you've done everything, try sailing.'*"

"Yeah. I'd say that's about right."

After he maneuvered through the moored boats, Owen pushed the fenders over the side then brought *Airship* to its slip at the dock. He and Riley tied off the lines and closed up the boat.

Owen pocketed the boat keys as the two of them stepped through the boarding gate and walked back up the ramp to the parking lot.

Riley reached for her car keys and turned toward her car, "What's that on my windshield?"

Owen squinted at her car, "It looks like a note. It's probably just a flier about a craft show or something going on in town."

As they got closer, it was apparent that it was not a flier. It was a note on her windshield.

When she got to her car, she read it out loud, *"STOP OR ELSE!"*

They were both in shock. Neither of them could speak. She looked around to see if the person who wrote it might still be in the parking lot. No one else was there.

"Damn it, Owen! We've got a really big problem here!"

"Wait a minute. Let's not jump to conclusions. Maybe it was some teenagers who put the message on your car by mistake."

"Yeah. That's possible, but what if it was Jase? Or, it could be Ella or my mother-in-law. Or, even your wife! It could be my daughters, for God sake."

"Let's just get rid of the message. We'll pretend it never happened."

"Oh, and that's going to solve our problem? I don't think so. Whoever did this has a pretty good idea that we were out on your boat just now, and they want us to stop what we're doing."

She grabbed the corner of the note to remove it from her windshield. It didn't budge. She tried again. Nothing. Owen offered to help, but he couldn't get it off either.

"It's stuck on with glue. It's dried on and won't come off."

"Crap! What am I going to do now? I can't drive home with that note in my face. Besides, what do I say to Jase when he sees it?"

"Does your auto insurance cover windshield damage?"

"I'm pretty sure it does. Why?"

"Because we can call a windshield replacement company, and they'll come and replace it for you right away. I'll call 'em for you if you want."

She opened her glove compartment and found the insurance card. She handed it to him, and he called the claims department. He asked them to dispatch a local glass service right away.

Within twenty minutes the service truck pulled up.

The driver stepped out and looked at Riley, "Are you Miss Reed?"

"Yeah. That's me. You're going to replace my windshield, right?"

He looked at the note glued to the windshield, "Looks like some kids had a weird sense of humor. Yes, Ma'am, I've got your new windshield on the truck. It won't take long to replace the bad one."

Relieved, she said, "Thank God! And, thank you. We'll just stay and watch. Okay?"

"Not a problem Ma'am. If it were me I'd go find out whoever did this."

20

The Phones

Jase was consumed with rage.

He was at work, but he wasn't focused on his job at all. He was certain his wife was seeing that asshole, Flynn, but he couldn't prove it. He had spent a lot of time just thinking about how he could catch her cheating on him. He'd checked the house telephone bills, Facebook, and the Internet, but found nothing.

Then, it hit him, "*How could I be so stupid?*"

He logged onto the Internet and connected to their cell phone account. He scanned the incoming and outgoing calls that Riley had made the past two months and there it was, Owen Flynn's phone number. There wasn't just one call between them, but more than a dozen.

The discovery of the phone calls merely confirmed what he'd worried about for years. His wife was having an affair with another man. He was outraged. His brain was spinning behind his eyes.

To him it was just a matter of dealing with the evidence. Should he call Riley and let her have it? Should he call his mother to tell her what he'd discovered? How about Ella or his daughters? He realized that his next step was critical. If he confronted her again, she'd just blame him for the problems in their marriage. If he told the family and made too much of her infidelity, it would reflect back on him as a bad husband. His mother would tell him, once again, that he never should have married Riley. It would all be his fault.

He was deep in thought, staring out his office window.

His eyes lit up when he realized, "*Owen Flynn!*"

That was his next step. He decided that Flynn had to be the solution. He had to find a way to drive him away from Riley. But, he had to be cautious. He didn't want to let on that he knew what was going on. He decided not to call Owen or make any further threats. Instead, he had to do something that would turn his threats into action without connecting it to him.

Jase dropped everything and began building his plan to end his wife's affair.

His work phone rang, "Hello, this is Jason Reed."

"Hi, Jase. It's Ella."

He sat back in his chair, "How's it goin' Ella?"

"I'm out back of the salon having a cigarette so they can't hear me. I've had it with my sister. I'm really pissed at her. I try to be nice at the salon, but it's not easy. She's cheating on you, but I can't prove it."

Jase listened to his sister-in-law go on about Riley and Owen. He considered telling her about the phone calls and his plan to end the affair. But, he was worried she might spill the beans.

He really didn't trust Ella at all. But, he realized that he had to take the risk. He needed her help.

He whispered through the phone, "Look, I'm going to tell you something, but you have to promise that you'll not say a word to anyone. Not your husband, not your mother, and, most of all, not to your sister."

She lied to him, "Of course not, darling. You know I can keep a secret better than anyone. I promise! So, tell me..."

He interrupted her, "I've been doing some investigating. I checked Riley's Facebook friends and posts, but nothing was there. I checked the text messages on her phone. Nothing there either. I checked the history on her Internet browser. I've even gone through her purse but found nothing at all. So, I finally decided to check her cell phone records at the phone company a little while ago, and there it was."

"What?"

"I found a dozen calls between Riley and Flynn over the past month alone."

"Oh my God, Jase! That's it! There can be no denying it now. They're having an affair. What're you going to do?"

"You've really got to promise that you'll not say anything to anyone. If she finds out that I have evidence, she and Flynn will do everything they can to hide from me. I've been putting together a plan that'll prove what's going on so she can't talk her way out of it. And, I want to teach that asshole boyfriend of hers a lesson he'll never forget."

"Yes, you've got to fix this for good. Have you told your mother?"

He shook his head, "No. Not at all. I know her all too well. If she found out about it, she'd run Riley down with her car. You know how my Mom hates her. I should've listened to her a long time ago. I'm paying the price for it now."

"I know, Jase. What're you going to do?"

"I don't have all the details yet, but I know that I need you to be a part of the solution. I'll let you know in a few days when I get it all ironed out."

"Okay, sweetheart. You know I'll do whatever it takes. I love you and want you and my nieces to be happy again. Call me as soon as you can."

Jase ended the call, "Thanks, Ella. I love you, too."

Ella was worried that Jase wouldn't tell her what his plan was. She knew him all too well and believed that he'd only let her help him if she did everything his way. She decided she needed to have her own plan to deal with her sister.

That evening, Ella drove over to her mother's.

Lisa looked through her front door window and was happy to see her favorite daughter on the front porch.

She opened the door then opened her arms, "Hello, my lovely daughter. Come on in."

Ella marched through the door and into the living room. She hated to visit her mother. The smell of cigarette smoke in the air was suffocating. She was tired of complaining that her step-father, Andy, must stop smoking so much. Her mother would just roll her eyes and agree, but nothing ever changed.

As Lisa slid onto her vinyl chair in the living room, Ella fell into the tufted brown sofa and propped her feet on the coffee table. Lisa never liked it when Ella did that, but she never told her to stop doing it. Never.

Lisa asked, "So, how're you doing?"

"Not good, Ma."

"Uh oh... What's wrong now?"

"Ma, I promised not to tell you this."

Lisa knew that Ella was a major, rumor mill all by herself. She couldn't keep secrets from anyone, especially her mother.

Ella continued, "I'm having a lot of anxiety over what I just heard about my sister from Jase."

She paused and stopped short of telling her any details.

Lisa started to get up from her chair, "Okay. So that's it? Well, thanks for stopping by my dear. Goodbye..."

"Ma! Wait! I need to tell you!"

Lisa fell back into her chair and smiled at her daughter, "All right. You've got my attention. Now, what am I not supposed to know?"

Ella took a deep breath, leaned forward then lied to her mother, "I knew all about this months ago, but I didn't want to tell you until now. Jase's been suspicious of Riley's behavior so he checked her phone records and found more than fifty calls between Riley and a guy by the name of Owen Flynn, one of her clients. Apparently, they're having an affair!"

Jumping from her seat, Lisa reacted, "Oh my God, sweetie! Are you sure about this?"

Ella sat back and planned her next words well. She wanted her mother on her side and needed to be careful what she told her. The last thing she wanted was for her mother to defend Riley.

"Look, Ma. You know I will never tell you something that's not true. I'm not making this up. Jase has clear evidence, and I believe him."

"I don't know, Dear. This is pretty serious stuff. Why would Riley risk everything to go on a fling with... what's his name, again?"

"Owen Flynn. He lives out on Windermere Place. He's twenty-five years older than Riley, for Christ sake."

"What? That's crazy. If she's having an affair with this guy, she's just plain stupid! We need to find out for real if this is true or not."

"Don't worry, Ma. I have a plan. Be sure you don't say a word to Riley. Okay?"

Lisa lied to her daughter, "I won't. This just needs to stop right away."

Ella talked with her mother a few more minutes then left for home.

Lisa spent a lot of time worrying about the news she'd just heard. She decided not to react too quickly. She needed to consider all the things that could possibly go wrong for her family.

First, she must be certain that Ella was telling the truth. Maybe it was just a rumor or maybe she and Riley had a fight and Ella wants to start a rumor about her baby sister. She's done it all her life.

But, Ella had told her there was hard evidence from Riley's phone records that she was having an affair. So, Lisa needed to find out the truth for herself. If the affair really was going on, she had to talk Riley out of it. She couldn't have people, and her friends in particular, gossiping all over town about her and her family.

Then there was the problem with this guy, Owen Flynn. Having an affair was one thing, but with some man twenty-five years older than her? It had to stop!

She needed a plan. If it was true that Riley was having an affair, Lisa had to find a way to stop it. And, she had to do it before it got out of hand. She had to call Riley first. She had to find out about the phone calls. What did they mean? Why so many calls if there was no affair?

She called her youngest daughter at home, "Hi, Ma."

"Hi, honey. How's work going?"

Immediately, Riley sensed a problem in her mother's voice. She decided to ignore it at first.

"Work is just great. Very busy, though. I need to take more breaks, or I won't last long. How are you?"

"Okay, I guess. I just talked with your sister. Is everything all right with you and Jase?"

Riley shook her head, "Ma! What makes you ask me that? Did Ella say something to you? She's been a pain in my ass lately making shit up about me. Don't listen to her."

"No, dear. She didn't say anything that you should be concerned about. She's always looking out for her little sister."

"So, she did say something to you about me. Damn it, Ma. Why don't you tell her that you don't want to hear crap about me from her?"

"Look, it's none of my business. There's just something about a bunch of phone calls between you and a man who comes into the salon for haircuts and manicures. People are talking."

Riley was outraged. Ella was spreading rumors about her and Owen. And, those rumors had made their way to her mother and probably to Jase. That meant trouble, a lot of trouble. She had to convince her mother that there was nothing to worry about.

"Ma! I make and receive phone calls every day from both men and women. They're all my clients. We make and change appointments all day long. I text people, too. Jesus, I got a text message from one of my clients at 3:00 in the morning last week. I'm on Facebook with a lot of people. Do you really think I'd have an affair with any of them? I'm not that dumb!"

Lisa lied to her daughter, "No, of course not. I believe you. It's just that people are connecting dots."

"People? You mean my sister! Tell me why she's trying to make trouble for me, Ma."

"That's not true, baby. Ella's only concerned for your happiness and wellbeing. And, so am I."

"Well here's one for you. Right now, you two are making me very unhappy! Goodbye, Ma."

The next day, Riley and Owen met again.

She was frantic, "We've got problems."

"We do? What problems, now?"

"It looks like someone's been checking up on me. It's either Jase or my sister. It's got to be Jase. He must have found a bunch of phone calls between us. He probably told Ella about them. Then, Ella told my mother. My Mom called me last night to ask me questions about us."

"Shit! This is not good. Julie's been suspicious, too. We've got to get out ahead of this before it gets worse."

"Yeah. Other than running off together, what should we do?"

Owen thought for a few seconds then told her, "The first thing we have to do is stop calling each other. I'm not going back to the salon for anything so that should help. Did you tell Crystal?"

"I did. She understood why, but she's very worried for us. By the way, I can't just stop calling you."

"We can still call, but we have to use different phones. I heard about these special cell phones. You can buy them at any drug store. They don't cost much, and there's no account information that can be monitored. You buy time cards that give you a set number of minutes for your calls."

"So, how do we use them?"

"A random phone number is already setup in the phone when you buy it. Once you enter the time card information you can make and receive calls just like any other phone. The difference is that no one can find out that you're doing it."

"That sounds like a good idea to me, if it works the way you say it does. Where do I go to get one?"

"I'll take care of it. I'll get one for each of us. I'll setup the phone numbers in speed dial so we don't have to remember the numbers."

"What if you call me while I'm having dinner with my family?"

"We'll have to make sure we don't do that. I think, too, we need to keep the phones off when we're not using them or when we don't want to get any calls. We have to be very careful, Honey."

"I'll hide my phone where Jase can't find it. It certainly won't go in my purse."

He agreed and told her he'd find a good place to hide his at home.

They kissed for a few minutes then agreed to leave for home.

The next day, Owen stopped at a CVS on his way to Portland. He bought two phones and two, 200-minute airtime cards. Before he left the store, there was just enough battery power for him to setup each phone with its airtime and enter the phone numbers into the speed dials.

When he got to his office, he setup the chargers for the phones and took out a note pad and pen.

He wrote on the pad, *'Things to hide: Haircuts at the Salon (done), Phone calls (done), Notes, Visits, what else?'*

Owen grappled with the *'what else?'* question. His relationship with Riley was becoming dangerous. A smart man would be able to figure out what to do to keep his affair a secret.

'But what if I miss something?'

21

The Sister

Crystal was finished with her last client at the salon.

She went out the back door and called Riley, at home making dinner.

Riley dried off her hands with a kitchen towel and picked up the phone, "Hello?"

"Hi, Riley, it's Crystal."

"Hi, my friend. What's goin' on?"

"I need to see you right away. Can you get away for a while?"

"Uh oh. What's wrong?"

"Look, I'm finished at the salon. You've got a big problem. I was about to go home when I decided we should talk. Can you meet me at The Dolphin Tavern?"

"Okay. I'll be there in five minutes."

Riley turned off the oven, grabbed her purse, and headed out to her car.

She didn't say a word to Jase on her way out.

When she arrived at the tavern, Crystal was already there.

Riley went in and joined her friend at a booth near the front window. Crystal was halfway through her first Shipyard Ale.

She looked up at Riley, "Hi. I hope I didn't interrupt anything."

"Nope. Not a problem. Tell me. What's wrong?"

"You know I love you as a friend. I don't want to see you get hurt. But, you have to know what's been going on behind your back."

"This is about my sister. Isn't it?"

"Yes, it is. You've got to know that I'm not snooping around or anything. But, I hear stuff I shouldn't be hearing."

Riley slid forward on her elbows, "I know you too well, Crystal. I know you wouldn't make shit up. So, do I have to beat it out of you? What's going on?"

"Ella's been telling her clients about you and Owen. Something about lots of phone calls between you two. And..."

Riley straightened up, looked at the ceiling, and cried out, "That bitch! What the fuck is she doing? We don't need any more drama at the salon. And, family business is no one else's business. Damn it!"

"I'm so sorry this is happening to you. I really can't say anything to Ella. It's none of my business. But, I can't just stand by and watch you get hurt."

Riley started to cry, "Crystal, you know that I've always been honest with you. And, you know that things haven't been going well between Jase and me. But, things are getting worse. Am I having an affair with Owen? The answer is that I just don't know. We've been close these past few weeks. I like him. No, I like him a lot. He makes me happy when we're together. He believes in me. He listens to me. He wants to know everything about me. And, I want to know everything about him. He's the very opposite of my husband."

Crystal shook her head, "I've watched you for years now. You haven't been happy at all. At first, I thought it was Lauren's health. But, a few years ago, I started to get the impression it was Jase. He's never really treated you well at all."

"No. He hasn't. And, now I don't know what to do."

Crystal joked, "Well, the first thing we have to do is kill your sister."

Riley smiled at her suggestion, "That's a little over the top, don't you think?"

"That's what I'd do. Without hesitation. But, seriously, Ella cannot be doing this in your salon. People are already taking sides. That's not good. You have to stop her."

"I already had it out with her, but, apparently, it didn't do any good. Nothing's changed. In fact, from what you're telling me, it's getting worse."

"Then you have to get rid of her."

Riley was silent for a moment then agreed "Yeah. She has to go. She'll be pissed off, and my mother will be furious. But, if I do this right, everyone will understand and agree that it's the only thing I can do."

"Do you need any help? I'll do whatever you need me to do. You know that. What do you think?"

"I think I want to have sex with Owen."

The next morning, Riley arrived at 7:00 to open the salon. She sat at her manicure desk nervously waiting for her sister to come in. She knew Ella would show up early, so they would be alone for at least an hour. Riley brought a cup of coffee with her to help ease the stress. It wasn't working.

Soon Ella walked in and greeted Riley, "You're here early."

She gave her sister a cold reply, "Hi, Ella."

"You okay?"

"No, not at all. I need to talk with you about something. Have a seat."

Ella put her purse and glasses on her counter then took a seat at Riley's desk.

Riley began, "I'm hearing stuff that bothers me a lot. You and I have had some problems lately and it's not getting any better."

Ella sat back and folded her arms across her chest, "There aren't any problems that I'm aware of. So, what are you saying?"

"You know full well there are problems. First off, you're telling your clients that I'm having an affair with Owen Flynn."

"Who told you that?"

"It's not important who told me. For years, I've personally overheard you gossiping all day long about some of the people in town. So, I know it's within the realm of possibility that you'd gossip about me behind my back. And, you and I already had it out over what you're telling Jase."

Ella got agitated, "What I say to people is no one else's business. Not even yours."

Riley got up from her desk and walked around to confront her, "I'm through with you and your lies. You've been trying to hurt me for years, and it's over."

"What do you mean it's over?"

"You're not to come into the salon anymore. You're fired."

"Bullshit! I'm not taking orders from you. I'm staying right here!"

Riley stared at her, "You're going to leave. I expected this from you so the police will be here any minute."

"What? You called the police on me? I'm your sister, for God sake."

"Yes, you are. And, it's too bad you didn't think about that before you started shooting your mouth off about my private life."

At about the same time, a police cruiser pulled up at the door, and an officer got out. He entered the salon and walked over to Riley and Ella.

He looked at his note pad then up at the two of them, "Good morning. I'm Officer Bolton. Which of you is Riley Reed?"

Riley picked her hand up, "I'm Riley. This is my sister, Ella McKenna."

He nodded to Ella then continued with Riley, "How can I help you, Ma'am?"

She explained to Bolton that she just fired her sister, and that she called the police in anticipation of a confrontation. She added that Ella was required to hand over the key to the salon door immediately.

Ella turned to the officer and pleaded, "Mister, ah... Bolton. I've done nothing wrong here. My little sister and I have had a small disagreement. That's all. We don't need you to get involved. Thanks."

Bolton looked at Riley, "Is this your salon Ma'am?"

"Yes. I own the salon."

"Does Miss McKenna work for you here?"

"Up to a minute ago, she did."

"So, you fired her?"

"That's correct. And, I need her to give me her key to the front door and leave."

He looked at Ella, "We don't want any problems here, do we Miss McKenna?"

"What are you saying? I have to leave?"

Bolton added, "And, we have to be adults here. As I just heard, the salon owner has just let you go, and she's asked you to leave now. Right now. Is that correct, Miss Reed?"

Riley nodded her head, "Yes. That's correct. She must leave right now and turn over her key on her way out."

Ella screamed at the cop, "She can't do this to me. I've done nothing wrong!"

"That's none of my business Ma'am. Please give Miss Reed her key."

Ella didn't move.

"Now, Miss McKenna!"

Ella went to her station, opened her purse, and removed the salon key from her keychain. She threw it at Riley.

The officer stepped in front of Ella, "Please Ma'am. Do not. I repeat. Do not become a problem here."

Ella screamed again at Riley, "You bitch! You fucking bitch. You're not going to be my sister anymore."

Riley didn't say a word, but just stared at her.

Bolton told Ella, "Now, miss. That doesn't help at all."

Ella settled down and obeyed the officer's request, "I'll need to get my stuff before I can leave. I have to go and get some boxes at home."

She started for the door when Riley called to her, "I have boxes and will pack up your things. I'll leave them on your front porch at the end of the day today. You're not welcome back at this salon. So, go home now! And, don't ever come back here again!"

Ella shouted back at Riley, "You're going to pay for this. Just wait and see what happens to you and that moron, Flynn!"

The next day, Riley and Owen met in Biddeford again. She joined him on the front seat of his car.

He took hold of her hand, "Are you all right? You were a bit stressed on the phone when you called this morning."

"I had to fire Ella yesterday."

"Uh oh. What happened?"

As tears began to fall, she paused a while then told him, "Crystal and I talked a couple of days ago about Ella's big mouth. She's been telling her clients at the salon that you and I are having an affair."

"Damn it! Why would she do that? At the very least, personal business has no place in your salon."

"Oh, that doesn't matter to Ella. She's always gossiping about someone in town. I'm surprised no one has attacked her in the parking lot yet."

"Maybe I should."

Riley didn't smile, "So... It didn't go well at all. She was really pissed off. She claimed she wasn't saying anything to anyone about us. That was a lie. I had no choice, but to let her go. My own sister, for God sake!"

He put his arm around her, "Hey, Honey. You did what you had to do. You can't have anyone in your salon, let alone your sister, telling personal stories about other people, especially you."

"That's not the worst of it. I had to have a cop there in case she got nasty and wouldn't leave. He helped her out the door. I packed up her shit and late last night dumped it on her front porch."

"What's wrong with that?"

"Well, before she left she threatened me. Actually, she threatened you and me. She said that we were going to pay for what I did to her."

"Fuck!"

22

The Book

Jase needed to go to the garage where his household tools were stored.

He was looking for some plumbers' putty to help stop a leak in the upstairs sink. He rumbled through his toolbox, but the putty wasn't there. He opened three drawers under the workbench and was about to give up when he found a book under some dirty rags.

The book was *"Nights in Rodanthe."*

He asked himself, *"What the Hell is going on here? This isn't my book, and I'm damn well sure it's not the girls' either. It has to be Riley's. But, why is she hiding it?"*

Puzzled over the mystery of the book, he flipped through several pages. He stopped here and there to read a sentence or two. It was obvious it was a romance novel. It had a soft tone to the words and the sentences ebbed and flowed together. The book was relatively new, but he could tell it'd been read already by the bend in some of the pages. Many of them had sentences or words that were underlined in red.

As he flipped past a particular page, he noticed something oddly different about it from the others. One by one he paged backward looking for that odd page. When he reached page 143 he discovered what had caught his eye a moment ago. The page number had been circled in red. He checked randomly at other pages in the book but found no other page numbers circled at all.

"Why would she circle page 143?"

He decided to read the whole page, as well as the pages before and after it.

There it was. On these three pages, the author described the two main characters as their feelings built up to make love for the first time.

Jase's eyes sprang open, "Goddamn it!"

Riley was in the middle of cooking a roast beef dinner when Jase thundered into the kitchen. The book was tightly gripped in his right hand.

He threw it on the kitchen table and yelled at Riley, "So, you've got something really going on here with that asshole, Flynn! Don't you?"

Startled, Riley straightened up from the oven and shouted back at him, "What's your problem, now?"

"Why did you hide this book in the back of my workbench drawer?"

She took the book out of his hand, flipped through a few pages then lied to him, "Look, I have no idea what you're talking about. I've never seen this book before in my life."

"You're a lying bitch. You know that?"

"Jase. Settle down. I didn't hide any book, and that's the truth."

He lost his patience and went after her, "You circled page 143. It's about two people making love. So, somehow you see yourself and Flynn in this story? Making love?"

"If that's true why would I be so stupid as to hide it in your workbench?"

Riley knew she'd been caught. She actually was stupid for putting the book in that drawer. She had to continue denying it.

Jase was losing his mind. He was more convinced than ever that his wife was having an affair with Flynn.

He grabbed hold of Riley's right wrist and twisted it nearly halfway around. She bent forward in an attempt to get loose.

But, he tightened his hold causing her to scream out in pain, "Jase! What the Hell are you doing? You're hurting me. Let go!"

With her left hand, she tried to set herself free, but it was no use.

He squeezed even harder, pushed his face into her right ear, and spit out his words, "I'll let go as soon as you tell me the truth!"

He brought his free hand up and wrapped both around her neck. He began to tighten his hold, choking her.

He raised his voice even louder, "I told you and that asshole that there would be consequences if you two kept seeing each other. Well, how does this feel?"

The noise had alerted their daughters doing homework up in their bedrooms. They ran downstairs into the kitchen. They were shocked to find their father choking their mother, pushed up against the refrigerator.

Kelly ran up to her father, grabbed his arms, and struggled with him, "Daddy! What are you doing to Mom? Let her go!"

Nothing happened. He wouldn't let go of Riley's throat.

Lauren jumped in to help her sister, "Daddy! Stop it! You're hurting Mom! Stop it now!"

Jase's rage subsided as he realized his daughters were scared at what he was doing to their mother. He let go of Riley's throat. He fell onto a kitchen chair and hung his head. He bent forward, placed his elbows on the table, and wiped his face with a kitchen towel.

He felt both helpless and angry at his wife. There seemed to be no solution to his problem. Riley was adamant that she was not having an affair with Flynn even though he had clear evidence that she was. His threats, and now his attacks, had no effect.

It was time to step up his daughters' emotions and turn them against their mother.

The three women cried. Riley took a chair out from under the kitchen table and dropped onto it, placing her head in her hands. She couldn't stop crying.

Lauren turned to her father and demanded, "What's going on? Why are you trying to hurt Mom?"

"Because your mother is nothing but a whore! She's having sex with another man. This guy's trying to steal your mother away from us, for God sake. And, she fired your aunt to cover up her sins!"

As her jaw dropped open, Kelly turned to her mother and yelled, "What? This can't be true! Ma, you can't be doing this to us! And, to Aunt Ella, too?"

Riley picked up her head and leaned across the table at Jase, "What are you doing to me, and to our girls? I'm not a whore. I'm not having an affair with anybody. No one is stealing me away from you. No one! This is all in your mind, damn it."

Riley was now so angry at Jase and her daughters that she decided to get out of the house for a while. As she started around the table to get to her purse and keys, Kelly grabbed them, preventing her mother from escaping.

"What's this all about? Give me my keys. I'm going out!"

"No, you're not, Ma. I want you to tell us the truth."

Riley was afraid. She'd been lying to her husband and now to their daughters. She'd ventured into a space in which she'd never been before.

Absent any more words, she stormed out of the kitchen and up the stairs to her bedroom, slamming and locking the door behind her. She spent the rest of the night crying in bed.

Jase spent the night on the living room couch.

The next day, Riley called Owen.

"Hey, you. How are you? That bitch of a sister giving you anymore trouble?"

She choked up, "This time it's not my sister that's the problem. It's Jase."

"What has he done now?"

"He tried to kill me last night."

"What? He did? What the Hell happened?"

"The book. He found it and went through it. When he got to the circled page, he read about the love making. He came after me claiming that it was really about you and me. I denied everything, but he could tell I was lying. He got very emotional and demanded I tell him the truth. He lost all control and went after me. He grabbed me around the neck and squeezed my throat. He wouldn't let go. I couldn't breath and started choking. My daughters caught it all. If they hadn't stopped him, I'm sure he would have killed me."

"Damn him! Did you call the police?"

"No. But, I should have."

23

The Mother-in-Law

Ella was not going to take it from that *'Goddamn sister'* of hers.

She was on her way into town when she used her car phone to call Jase's mother.

Caryn picked up, "Hello?"

"Hi, Caryn. It's Ella."

"Hey. How are you, sweetheart?"

Ella skipped the small talk, "Not good. Not good at all."

"Uh oh. What's wrong?"

"Do you have a minute? I need to talk with you. It's really important."

"Why sure, Ella. Of course. Come on over right away."

It took Ella about six minutes to drive over to Caryn's house. She parked on the street then walked up the front porch stairs. Caryn didn't give her a chance to ring the doorbell.

The front door opened, "Come on in, darlin'. Is everything all right?"

Ella moved quickly into the living room and before she sat down answered Caryn's question, "No. Everything's not all right. Yesterday, my sister fired me at the salon. She's such a bitch!"

"Why what happened?"

Ella lied, "I don't know. I didn't do anything wrong. She's making things up. She even had the police there claiming I might hurt her. I couldn't sleep at all. Damn her!"

Caryn moved to sit with Ella, in tears, on the couch, "Tell me what's goin' on."

"My bitch of a sister came up with some crazy idea that I was spreading shit about her. But all she's been doing is having an affair with... "

Caryn squealed, "An affair!? Damnit! With who?"

"It's one of her manicure clients. His name is Owen Flynn."

"Owen Flynn? From town? I know who he is. He lives out on Windemere Place in one of those big ass houses on the water. Right?"

"That's what I've heard. People tell me his family's been around here for, like, a hundred years or so."

Caryn corrected her, "No. Make that almost three-hundred years. Somebody told me they came over on the Mayflower or something."

"Well, whatever. Riley's been after him for a while, now. Every time he came into the salon, I saw them smiling at each other. They spent hours on the bench outside assuming I couldn't see them. But, I did. They were always laughing, probably making jokes about your son."

Caryn choked her words out, "Goddamn her! Does Jase know anything about this?"

Ella lied, again, "I told him I suspected something was going on, but he did nothing about it."

Enraged, Caryn raised her voice, "My fucking son has no balls at all. I knew she was going to be a problem, and I've told him so for years. We've got to stop this and now."

Ella cautioned, "Let's be careful here. I think Riley's the one we have to deal with. But, I won't talk to her anymore. Not after last night!"

"I'll take care of it."

"Oh? Like what?"

"That'll be my secret. You go along now and don't say anything to anyone about this. I'll take care of your little sister."

"Thanks, Caryn. I knew I could count on you. Let me know what happens. Okay?"

Caryn lied, "I will, sweetie. Thanks for letting me know about this."

They both got up together and hugged each other. Ella turned and headed back out to her car.

Ella was pleased that she'd just met her objective. Caryn was to bring Riley down and Ella would avoid any blame for whatever happened to her little sister.

As soon as Ella drove away, Caryn dialed Riley's cell phone.

Riley recognized her Mother-in-Law's number and avoided any pleasantry, "Hello, Caryn."

With her voice shaking in anger, Caryn said, "I just heard some very disturbing news, and I need to talk with you about it."

Riley stopped her, "Just a minute. I'm in the salon and need to go out back."

She excused herself from her client, got up from her desk, and went out the back door. She closed it behind her and got back on the phone with Caryn.

"Okay. What's the problem?"

"You little shit. You know damn well what the problem is! I've just been told you're having an affair with one of your clients, Owen Flynn."

Riley fell back against the wall of her salon, "What are you talking about!? Where did you ever hear such a thing?"

Caryn lied to Riley, "There are a lot of people in town who know what's going on. It's been happening for months, now, in your salon right in front of everybody."

"So, let me get this straight. You say I'm having an affair with one of my clients in front of my customers? That's just nuts, Caryn. I think you need to go back to bed or something."

Pissed at Riley's response, she screamed at her over the phone, "You know what I mean. I told my son not to marry you. You were just a big flirt hoping to catch any man you could. My son fell for it, and now you're just taking it to the next step. Aren't you?"

"Absolutely not! You bitch!"

She hung up on Caryn.

24

The Device

Jase was not deterred by Riley's behavior in the kitchen.

He spent a good part of his day at work trying to find a way to prove to his daughters that their mother was a cheater and, if not stopped, would destroy their family.

He checked the cell phone account again but found that the calls between Riley and Owen had stopped. He knew that Ella would have told him if Flynn had returned to the salon, but she hadn't mentioned it for a while. She also would have told him if she'd even seen Flynn around town, but nothing.

Was it possible that the affair was over? Jase didn't believe that for a second. Nevertheless, he was worried that people in town might learn about his problems with Riley. His family, and even his friends, might think that he had done something wrong, and that the problems in his marriage were caused by him, not Riley. He couldn't let that happen. To Jase, it was more important to ensure that Riley was seen as the villain than it was to correct their problems.

Jase devised a plan that would produce irrefutable evidence that Riley had been unfaithful to him.

He needed to find out where Riley and Owen were spending their time together. Then he'd be able to record their encounters and share it with the family. Especially with his girls.

But, he couldn't just follow Riley around town. He had a job and couldn't get away. Besides, Riley would recognize his car anyway. And, he couldn't ask a co-worker to follow her around, that would expose him to rumors he didn't need. He had to find a way to monitor her movements.

He decided to check the Internet and Googled "tracking services." Besides companies like FedEx, UPS, and DHL, it showed nothing that he was looking for.

Not discouraged, he tried again and entered the words "tracking device," and, bingo, the search returned with several responses. He scanned the list and found a "GPS Vehicle Tracking" device. He quickly read the details and saw that it was magnetic so it could be hidden under Riley's car. The device could also communicate with an Internet app that provided times, dates, and places where her car had gone. It even provided a map that could locate her exact location in real-time.

It was perfect!

He called the distributor and ordered it, along with the reporting app and live mapping tool. He requested expedited delivery to his work address for the next day.

Jase told himself, *"I've got you now, you bitch!"*

The next day, Jase was at work and received the order at his desk. He opened the box and read the installation instructions. He inserted two batteries into the back of the device and turned it on to test it. A small green light came on. It was ready to go. He read the download instructions to insert the reporting app and mapping tool onto his cell phone.

He told his co-workers that he had to go out for an hour.

He got in his car and drove into Kennebunkport. He knew where Riley parked her car so he pulled up next to it. He looked around to make sure no one saw him then bent down and found a place to attach the device. He turned it on. The green light brightened. Jase attached it just under her passenger door.

There. It was all set.

He was pleased with himself, proving once again that he was 'the smartest man on the planet.'

The next day, Riley was finished at the salon. She turned off the lights and locked the door behind her.

She headed for her car on the other side of the parking lot, got in, and started the engine. She backed out and pointed the car toward the exit.

On her way, she failed to avoid the rather large pothole in the parking lot that had become a painful irritation over the past few months. Her car jolted in and out of the hole.

The sound of metal hitting the ground under her car startled her.

"That damn pothole has broken something under my car."

She stopped, shifted into 'park,' and got out to examine the damage. The sun was sinking fast, but she still had enough light to see under the car. There, just in back of the rear axle on the passenger side was a black box that appeared to have fallen from under the car. She reached underneath and retrieved it. She turned it around in her hands and was pleased to see that it hadn't been badly damaged, just slightly scraped on one side.

Oddly though, the box was clean and looked brand new. Her car had seen four brutal Maine winters, and she rarely got her car washed. Upon further examination, she read the product information label on the back.

"What the Hell is this? Trans-Global Tracker? A tracking device?"

Her next thought was of Jase. He was out to get her and was going to use GPS to find out where she was all the time. Things couldn't get much worse.

With the device still in her hand, she got back in her car and continued toward the exit. Then it hit her.

She slammed on the brakes and backed up about ten feet. She pulled into a parking space next to a Camry with Idaho plates. She got out with the GPS in her hand and looked around to see that she was alone. She was. So, she bent down next to the Camry and stuck the device to the bottom of the car frame.

"That'll certainly add some fun to Jase's day!"

As she got back into her car and moved toward the exit, she proclaimed at the top of her lungs,

"Fuck you, my love. Fuck you!"

25

The Hack

A few days later, Owen went into the office on the first floor of his house.

He turned on his iMac then started to log-in to his email account.

But, the computer rejected his password. He tried again. But, the email server still didn't recognize the password. Something was wrong.

As any experienced engineer would do, he decided to re-boot the computer and start over.

Instead of waiting for the re-boot to complete, he went back into the kitchen for another cup of coffee. He grabbed the paper off the floor of the front porch and checked the headlines. Nothing important going on, so he took the paper and his coffee back to his office.

After another three minutes, his computer was back up and ready to go. He tried to log-in to his email again, but he got the same error. He knew he hadn't changed the password in months, but, considering the possibilities, he tried logging in with his old password. Same problem.

He went upstairs and found Julie in the bathroom finishing her shower.

"I know this is a stupid question, but have you changed the email password on my computer?"

"Now why in Hell would I do that?"

"Sorry. Just checking. I can't seem to get into my email. I'll see if anything else is going on."

He went back downstairs to his computer, settled into his office chair, and leaned forward with his elbows on the desk. He slid his mouse over his 'Important Docs' folder and double-clicked the left button.

Suddenly every file in the folder started opening, overlaying one after another on the screen. He tried to stop it, but to no avail. Finally, after a hundred and thirty-two documents and spreadsheets laid opened on his display, it stopped.

"Holy shit!"

He tried another folder, but he got the same reaction. And, he couldn't close anything on his computer's desktop, either.

At whit's end, it was time to call in the cavalry.

He hit his phone's speed dial and waited for a familiar voice to pick up.

"Hey, Owen. What's up?" asked Bill Stafford.

"I'm going crazy over here with my computer. Something bad's happened. Could be a virus, but Apple computers don't typically behave like this. I need the help of my local systems engineer. Can you come over right away?"

"I just got out of the shower so it'll take me about a half hour before I can stop by. That okay?"

"Of course. Sorry I'm so screwed up about this. But, nothing like this has ever happened before."

Bill tried to calm him down, "Hey, my friend. Not to worry. You know, better than I, that every computer glitch can be fixed. I'll be there as fast as I can."

When Bill arrived, Owen was waiting for him at the door, "Thanks for coming so fast, Bill. I really need your help. Two more minutes and this computer of mine would've been in pieces out on the front lawn."

Bill laughed, "I guess I'm here in the nick of time, as usual. Let's go see our patient."

They headed into the office. Bill sat at the desk and stared at the hundreds of files that were open on the display in front of him.

"Holy shit!"

Owen chuckled, "My words exactly. Can I get you a cup of coffee?"

"Thanks, my friend. Yes, as usual, black with a bucket of Bailey's."

"Coming right up."

Bill studied the screen, tried to open another folder, and got the same result. As with Owen, he attempted to close files, but that didn't work either. Instead of re-booting he tried to shut down the computer, but the computer didn't comply. The only action available to him then was to physically unplug the computer. He pulled the power cord out of the back of the iMac and waited ten seconds. He plugged the power cord back in and waited while the computer ran through its startup process.

Finally, the display was clear of all the files that had been opened so the screen displayed only the twenty or so icons and folders that Owen had placed there.

He avoided opening any document folders, but instead opened the Utilities folder. He selected the Disk Utility and began his examination.

After nearly two hours, Bill called Owen back into the office.

He told him the bad news, "You've been hacked!"

Owen's jaw dropped, "I've been hacked? You mean like someone in China has gotten into my computer?"

"I have no idea where this is coming from. It could be China, Russia, Chicago, or right next door. I have no way of knowing. What I do know is that whoever did it found it easy to get into your computer."

"How?"

"Well, to start with, your firewall was not on, so the gate was wide open. They just walked right in. And, you didn't encrypt any of your data either. They were able to read your stuff like it was a book."

"Jesus, Bill. What did they see?"

"Everything! They got your Social Security number, all your passwords and user IDs, your bank accounts and their balances, your college transcript, every document the Army ever issued to you, your military pension statements, your medical history, and more. They know more about you than you do."

"Shit. I'm in a lot of trouble here!"

Bill countered, "There's something here that's a bit strange, though."

"What do you mean?"

"They didn't do anything with the information they pulled out of your computer. They didn't take money out of your bank account or cancel your insurance policies. They didn't buy anything online at Amazon. Nothing. No action appears to have taken place with the data they found. It's like they just wanted to find out who you are, where you worked, and what you have."

"So, what should I do now?"

"Nothing, right now. Whoever did this, planted a virus on your disc. I removed it, so you can use your computer now without any more problems. I'm going to run a special program that will generate new passwords for you and produce a listing that we'll print out. I also activated your firewall and encrypted all your data."

"Christ, Bill. Thanks for helping me out here. But, it's odd that they planted that virus on my system."

"You're right. They could've just taken the data without your even knowing that they did it. It's as if they just wanted you to know what they did. They're telling you that they have the data and could do something with it if they wanted to. It's kind of like a threat."

Owen nodded his head, "Yeah. Kind'a like a threat."

26

The Codes

Later that afternoon, Riley called Owen.

"Hi, Honey. By the way, I've been calling you Honey for some time now. You okay with that?"

She smiled into her phone, "I like that a lot. At this point, calling you Owen seems a little weird."

"Agreed. I like the comfortable feeling I have being in love with you. So, Honey it will be."

"So, you love me? Did I just hear you say that?"

"Whoops. It just popped out. I didn't..."

"That's okay, Honey. It's been true for a while now, hasn't it? And, I have to tell you that I love you, too."

He breathed a sigh of relief, "I never thought that the first time we'd say that would be over the phone."

"Very romantic! But, let's do it again when we're face-to-face."

He agreed.

Then she added, "Not to change the subject, but I have to compliment you on getting these phones. I feel so much safer. I was beginning to worry that Jase was listening in on all our calls."

"I didn't think that was going to happen, but nowadays you never know. I need to tell you, though, that my computer was broken into last night."

"Broken into?"

"Not physically broken into but hacked. You know, like from China or somewhere."

"Why would someone want to hack into your computer from China?"

"It could be from anywhere. Probably not from China. But, it could even be Julie or Jase or your sister. Anybody."

"But, no one I know could hack into a computer."

"Whoever did it must have hired a professional. We'll probably never know who's behind it."

Riley pondered what Owen had just told her. Somebody had everything of his now. They could use it to blackmail either or both of them.

"All of this is getting to be very scary. Your computer being hacked. Jase trying to strangle me. And, yesterday, I found a GPS device under my car. I have to believe that Jase put it there to keep track of where I am and where I've been."

"Christ. So, he knows where you are right now?"

"Nope! I found it by accident in my parking lot and put it under a car with Idaho plates. My loving husband is going to go crazy for a while trying to find me somewhere in Boise."

"That was brilliant! But, it tells me we have to be especially careful. Who knows what he might try next? We should meet in Biddeford tomorrow. We need to talk about all this and not just over the phone."

Riley agreed, "I think you're right. Can you be there around 3:00?"

"Okay with me. Please be careful, Honey! I need you, and I love you. Stay safe."

"I love you, too."

Both of them were terrified at what might happen next.

It was 2:50 the next day when Riley pulled in behind Planet Fitness. She was early and scared. So many things were happening that were putting her on edge. She knew that the romance she enjoyed with Owen was being put to the test. This had better be for real, or she was in big trouble.

In another two minutes, Owen arrived and parked next to her. They smiled at each other through the car windows, but with a sense of fear. It was hard not to ask the question, *'Are we wrong?'*

He got out of his car then went and sat on Riley's passenger seat. At first, they didn't say a word. They barely looked at each other.

He spoke first, "I've thought a lot about what I might say to you today. First, I just need to ask you is everything all right?"

"Shit, no... This thing with your computer scares the Hell out of me. What if some in my family, or even yours, is behind it? They could blackmail both of us and force us to end this."

"I don't see how they could. First of all, there is nothing on my computer that could be used use to blackmail either of us. Even if they did try, I have no criminal record. I've done nothing illegal. I'm not a child molester or anything that I would be ashamed of. Besides, all my data is now encrypted and all my passwords have been changed.'"

"Is there anything at all in your computer about me or about us?"

"No. Of course not."

"If there was, we'd be finished."

Owen suggested that it was time they had a plan, "Look, I never give up on anything, no matter how difficult. It's my tragic flaw. And, right now I have a woman beside me that's worth fighting for. But, first we need to agree on a few things."

"Okay. Like what, exactly?"

"First and foremost, never admit to anything. If Jase or your family ask if you're in love with me, say, *'Absolutely not!'* If they show you something of mine that I left in your car by mistake, tell them *'I have no idea what that is or where it came from.'* If they show you photos of the two of us in my car, tell them, *'I don't know who that is, but it's not me in that car.'* In other words, deny everything."

"I don't know if I can pull that off, Honey. I'm a very bad liar. I'll need to practice. I'll bet Crystal would help me out."

He added, "And, we need to be careful about our communications. I think the phone thing is going to work out just fine. Be extra careful about where you keep it."

"Not to worry about that. I'm very good at hiding things."

He changed the subject, "Hey, you remember my suggestion about having secret codes. The 'love codes?'"

"Yes, you told me about page 143 in *'Nights in Rodanthe.'* I figured that out."

"What is it then?"

She smiled back, confident in her answer, "1-4-3 could be *'I need you'* or *'I want you'* or *'I miss you.'* But, most of all I think it means *'I love you.'*"

He moved closer to her, held her hands in his, and pulled them up to his lips.

He whispered, "Yes. And, I love you, too. There. I said it in person."

"How about a kiss… in person?"

They put their arms around each other then pulled close. This kiss was a special one. It was filled with the love they had just professed to each other. Their eyes were wide open. Both of their hearts were cheering. It was a kiss filled with a lot of affection, softness, and sweetness. It was becoming intimate now with a hint that more was on the way.

She pulled back a bit, "This is both beautiful and scary. We have to be certain about what we're doing. I love you. It took way too long for me to admit it. Now, there's no turning back for us."

"I know. It's more than just love. I feel like I could go on forever just loving you. I know deep in my heart that I always will."

Riley snapped back, thought for a bit then said, "So, here's a love code for you. How about *'1-4-3-4'*?"

He thought for a bit then asked, "*'1-4-3-4'*, eh? How about *'I love you...'* something or other?"

"How about *'more?'* As in, *'I love you more'*?"

"So, if I say *'1-4-3'* to you, you'll reply, *'1-4-3-4,'* back to me?"

"Yup. Then you'll say *'3-8.'* "

"Uh oh. You got me on this one."

"How about *'Not Possible.'*"

Owen fell back in his seat and sighed, "We're going to need a whole lot of 'love codes' to help us out. It'll be like trying to break the Japanese code."

"I don't have any idea what that means. But, I do know we need to hide better from everyone. We should write the codes in the notes that we leave for each other. We'd have to leave the doors unlocked so we can get at them."

"And, let's hope that Jase and his family don't find the cards and break the code, or we're fucked."

"Yeah. And, Julie too."

They kissed and said their goodbyes.

He whispered to her, "1-4-3."

Riley smiled back and whispered, "1-4-3-4."

He countered, "3-8."

Owen got out of her car and back into his.

He opened his window just as she opened hers, "I'll have more codes for you to figure out next time. Until then, stay safe. 4-4!"

Before he left, Owen found himself looking around the parking lot. He had a strange feeling someone was watching them.

27

The Tires

Two days later, Owen finished work a little early.

It was just about 5:00 and he knew, it being Friday, that tourists would be filling up the highway soon.

He took the elevator to the garage floor and headed for his car. He rounded the last pillar and took out his keys.

But, he noticed something odd. His car seemed to be sunken in the concrete, as if it was in a hole. The light in the garage was dim so he couldn't quite make out what the problem might be.

He unlocked and opened the driver door which turned on the overhead light in the front seat. With better lighting, he was able to see the problem.

The driver side front tire was flat.

"Damn!"

He threw his briefcase onto the front seat then moved to the back. He opened the trunk to retrieve the spare tire, jack, and tire iron.

"What the fuck?" he yelled, as he noticed that the back tire was flat, too.

He walked around to the passenger side and found that both its tires were flat.

He shook his head and thought, *"Someone has slashed all my tires. Why? Just more crap to deal with."*

He took out his special phone and called Riley.

"Hi, Honey. I was just about to call you. How are you?"

"My tires have been slashed!"

"Which one?"

"All of them."

Riley was shocked, "What? At the airport?"

"Yeah. I was about to leave work and found my wheels just sitting on the concrete floor. My car can't move."

"Uh oh! Is this about us again?"

"I don't know. It could just be some local kids up here in Portland pulling off a high school prank."

She agreed, "I hope that's all it is..."

Suddenly, three rows away, the sound of screeching tires interrupted Owen's call to Riley. He pulled the phone away from his ear and looked toward a green, pickup truck speeding out of the garage. He couldn't read the license plate number. All he saw was a yellow stripe across the tailgate. The truck turned the corner and headed out the exit.

He put the phone back up to his ear.

"Owen? Honey? You there? Owen?"

He finally answered her, "Sorry. I'm still here. Do you know anyone who drives a green pickup truck with a yellow stripe across the tailgate?"

"What's that all about?"

"Someone in a pickup truck just flew out of here in a really big hurry. I have a feeling whoever was driving it had something to do with my tires."

"Did you get the plate number?"

"No. He was too far away. All I could see was that it was dark green with a yellow stripe across the back."

"Why do you say, *'he'*?"

"I don't know. I assume it was a man. But, it could just as well have been a woman. I couldn't tell for sure either way."

"With all this shit going on, someone's trying to intimidate us. And, I'd say they're doing a pretty good job of it so far. You think it's the same person who hacked your computer?"

"Maybe so. I have no idea. This is all a mystery to me. But, you're right. Someone's out to make life miserable for us. For now, I need to get some new tires."

"What're you going to do? Your car is just a chunk of iron right now."

"I'll call Andy Warren at his garage to come and get the car. I'll have him bring it to his place in town and put some new tires on it."

"What'll you tell Julie?"

"Hey, some high school kids got into the garage and slashed the tires on a bunch of cars. I'll have her meet me at Warren's garage after I get there."

"How do you know it wasn't someone in Jase's family that did this?"

"I don't know that it was. And, I don't know that it wasn't. There's no way to find out, either. We can't just ask Jase or anyone else without giving us away."

Riley started to cry, "Honey. I'm scared as Hell, right now"

Owen agreed, "Yeah. Me, too."

He called Julie, "Hello?"

"It's me. I've got a problem with my car. I'm still in the garage at work."

"What's the matter?"

He lied to her, "Apparently, some high school kids went on a rampage and slit the tires on a bunch of cars in the parking garage. They ruined all four of mine."

"Goddamn it! These fucking kids have no respect for other people's property. What are you going to do now?"

"I've called Warren's Garage in town. Andy will tow my car in and put new tires on for me. It should only take a couple of hours. I should have it back by noon tomorrow."

"How're you getting home tonight?"

"I'll go back in Andy's tow truck. I'll call you when I get there, and you can come pick me up."

"For Christ sake, Owen! I don't have time to go running around town looking for you. Can't you just get a ride home from one of your sailing buddies?"

He hung up on Julie and, later, took a cab home.

28

The Moment

The next Saturday, Julie was away, again, with her sister.

Owen showered and dressed quickly. He and Riley were going to meet at *Airship*.

The sun was just up, a soft breeze was blowing, and the sky was already a deep blue. A perfect day had dawned for them.

At 8:30, he headed down to the yacht club to ensure everything was ready. On his way there, he stopped at Dannah's boutique and purchased a beautiful, one-of-a-kind, silver necklace. He also found two red roses from the back of the shop. He knew Dannah's always had unique gifts just for lovers.

At the yacht club, he boarded *Airship*, went below, and turned on the circuit breakers. He moved into the forward berth to check that everything was ready. He placed the roses on the pillows and the necklace, still in its velvet case surrounded by a satin ribbon, at the foot of the bed.

He looked in the head to make sure the towels and sink were clean. He opened the fridge to see that the Chardonnay was cooling.

He was nervous. He felt like a teenager. He stood at the mirror and checked his hair. He drank some water to wash away the dryness.

"Hello? Anybody down there?"

Owen stuck his head up, out of the hatch, "Hey there, my lovely lady!"

"Why, thank you, skipper. What's goin' on?"

"Not much. It looked like a perfect day to go sailing. How about you? Wanna' join me?"

"I moved all my appointments, so I could do something exciting today. Going sailing with you is the most exciting thing I can think of. Let's do it!"

Owen spent time just staring at her. She was more beautiful today than at any time before. Her highlighted, blonde hair flowed perfectly down and over her shoulders. She had put on makeup but knew she didn't need it. Her skin was deeply tanned, soft, and smooth. She was wearing dangling silver earrings. Her yellow sundress covered her shoulders with short, lace-trimmed sleeves. The front of her dress was open from her neck down, showing more cleavage than necessary. But, that was by design.

Owen loved the sight he saw.

He went topside and stepped into the cockpit. He gave her his hand and helped her onto the deck. She jumped into his arms in the cockpit then below to the galley.

When she reached the bottom of the ladder, she heard him whisper, "Hey you?"

She turned to his voice and was surrounded by his arms. She slowly slid hers around his waist.

They pulled closer to each other then started to kiss. At first, the kisses were short and gentle. Owen kissed her neck. She kissed his cheeks. They stopped and took the time to look into each other's eyes. They moved their lips closer.

She pulled back and told him, "I love you, mister."

He resumed his short kisses, "And, I have never... loved anyone... as much as I... love you."

He ended with a lingering kiss across her lips. They parted. The passion they had for each other consumed them. They held tight, pressing their bodies ever closer.

"I have some Chardonnay in the fridge."

"Why? You wanna' get drunk?"

"No way! I just thought we could have a few sips and relax a bit."

"All right. Just a few sips and no more. I need you sober."

She walked through the galley, into the lounge, and sat on one of the tufted cushions. While he opened the wine, she positioned her body for her most appealing look. Her yellow dress was short, so she crossed her legs allowing him to get a good look at the tan on her thighs.

He walked the two glasses of wine into the lounge. She was smiling fully as he sat close to her. He handed her half a glass of wine. They kissed quickly, again. They both took a short sip of wine. Then, another.

He couldn't help but notice her legs, "You really know how to drive me crazy. Don't you? You're incredible."

"Who me? I'm just a simple homemaker out on a date."

He put his glass on a coaster on the teak table and looked up at her, "I would love for you to be the maker of my home."

"So, would I, my love. So, would I."

She put her glass on the table next to his. She cupped his right hand in both of hers and pulled them close to her. She ran her lips across his fingers.

He slowly slid his left hand across her right cheek, over her ear, and stopped at the back of her head.

His lips gently touched hers, "Can I show you something?"

"Uh oh! What are you up to now?"

He stood and took her hand, "Come with me."

They stepped through the entrance to the forward berth. There, on the bed, were the two, bright-red roses resting on the pillows and a black velvet box at the foot of the bed.

"Honey... you are very romantic. I just love red roses. What's in the case?"

"There's only one way to find out."

Riley picked the case up and pulled the ribbon to the side, "This is a little heavy, there, mister. I know… it's a set of batteries. Right?"

"Boy, you really are a very smart young lady. Yes, they're four 'D' cells."

She laughed then slowly opened the case.

The necklace inside was beautiful, "Oh my God, Owen. This is absolutely amazing. You know you shouldn't have done this. Okay, enough with that. Now, help me put it on!"

She removed it from its case, unclipped the latch, and handed it to him. She turned around, pulled her hair aside, and bent her head down. He spread the two ends out to either side of her head and gently drew them to the back of her neck. He connected the two ends behind her and let the necklace hang down to her chest.

Riley looked down then stepped to the mirror in the head, "Owen, Honey, this is absolutely gorgeous! I love it! I'm sorry that I…"

"Stop! This is for us. It's not a ring, but a token of our love. Think of it as a commitment to each other. I want you to wear it only when we're together, here on the boat. Agreed?"

"You bet your ass, sailor! I was going to suggest it stay here for safe keeping, just in case."

She went to the side of the bed and picked up the roses before laying on the bed. She rested her head on the pillows and handed one of the roses to Owen. He knelt onto the bed then laid down beside her. With his rose in hand, he slowly passed its fragrant petals across her nose. She smiled at the gesture.

They kissed. It was not an ordinary kiss at all. It was filled with anticipation of the morning ahead. They looked into each other's eyes as they had so many times before, but this time it was different. There was intense excitement in the air.

She pushed him onto his back then climbed over him, straddling him at his waist. With a hunger in her lips, she kissed him. He put his arms around her and pulled her down closer. Suddenly they felt the exhilaration of their two bodies totally pressing against each other for the first time.

His lips barely touched hers. The sensation sent a pulse through her body. She shuddered and let out a soft sigh.

Her lips parted as he opened his. His tongue gently slid across the inside of her lips. She was in a trance. The pleasure of the moment took over. She was in his arms, and he was caressing her with a love and affection she'd never felt before. Her head was spinning, and she was beyond all rational thought.

She wanted him. He wanted her. It was time.

Jase's work phone rang.

"Hello, this is Jason Reed. How can I..."

Betsy interrupted, "Hi, Jason. It's Betsy down at the salon"

"Oh. Hi, Betsy. What's up?"

Without answering, she continued, "Do you know where Riley is?"

"Why? Is there a problem at the salon?"

"Yes. The second sink is leaking again. She was scheduled to come in today, but all her appointments have changed."

"Changed? She told me she didn't have any appointments this morning, so she was going shopping."

Sensing she'd stumbled onto an issue between Riley and Jason, Betsy tried to exit the call, "No problem, Jason. I'm sure there's a good explanation. Thank…"

Agitated, Jason continued, "I tried her cell phone a couple of times, but she's not answering. I just figured she was too busy."

"I'm sure you're right. Don't worry. I'll have her check in with you the minute she gets in."

Jase faked agreement, "Yeah, you're right. Thanks, Betsy. I'll get over to the salon after work tonight and fix the sink... again."

She smiled, "Yeah. Thanks, Jason."

When he hung up, he walked into his boss's office to explain that he had a family emergency and needed to leave.

His boss pointed out the window, "Okay, Jase. Now, get your ass outta' here. We'll cover for you. Now, get!"

With that, Jase left his office and ran to his car. He pulled out his cell phone and opened the GPS app. After a few clicks, a map came on-screen with a blinking red dot indicating its whereabouts. The dot was moving but the names of the streets and towns didn't make any sense. He expanded the map to see where she was. Riley's car was moving through Ohio.

"Shit! She's in Ohio? But, she was at home just a few hours ago."

He then triggered the function that told him the location history of her car. It reported that she left Kennebunkport two days ago on her way west.

"Okay! This GPS isn't working. It's a piece of shit!"

Since he was already out of the office, he decided to find Riley on his own. He raced out of the company lot toward Kennebunkport. He was convinced that she was with Flynn and was determined to find them, probably at his house.

After breaking every speed limit along the way, he slowed onto Western Avenue. He had found out from a friend that the Flynn's house was on Windermere Place. At Dock Square, he turned right onto Ocean Avenue, passing the Arundel Yacht Club.

He didn't see Riley's car hidden in the yacht club parking lot.

After a few minutes, he turned off Shore Road onto Windemere Drive. He slowed to five miles an hour, looking both sides of the road for her car. He traveled the full length of Windermere but didn't find it.

He turned around to go back, *"She must be parked in his garage."*

There was no way he could get into Flynn's garage, so he parked at the bend and waited for her to appear. It was 10:30 in the morning.

By a little after 11:00, he was frustrated. He gave up his lookout for Riley and started back toward his job. He passed the yacht club again, but still didn't notice her car parked there.

Nor did he have a clue as to what was about to happen aboard *Airship.*

Owen smiled as he moved Riley off of him. Then he slid on top of her, kissed her left ear then barely slipped his tongue inside her mouth. His kisses moved from her ear, down her neck, and to her chest. Her breathing got heavy as her heart beat faster.

Softly, she began to moan, "I've wanted this day for so long."

He stopped for a moment and looked down at her, "I love you, Riley Reed. And, I don't think you should be wearing this dress on my sailboat."

"And, why not? Don't you like it?"

"Oh, I love it. The point is that when you're on a sailboat, you're either in a bathing suit or you're naked. So, what's it going to be?"

"Okay. I apologize. I didn't know the rules. But, I must admit I didn't bring my bathing suit."

She adhered to the shipboard rules and let him remove her dress, along with the rest of her clothes.

Naked, she stood at the foot of the bed. Her eyes smiled down at him.

Owen could barely speak, "You are the most beautiful sight I've ever seen."

She extended both arms, begging him to hold her. He accepted, took both her hands, and stood in front of her. They pulled together then wrapped their arms around each other again.

While he held her, Riley unbuttoned his shirt. Then pulled it over his shoulders and dropped it to the floor. Next, she yanked his belt buckle open and pulled the belt out through the loops in his jeans.

She pushed him back onto the bed and popped his left shoe off. Then his right. Next, she grabbed both legs of his jeans and pulled them off. She pulled his boxers down and dropped them on the deck floor.

Before she was finished, she slowly slid her hands up both of his now naked legs.

The smiles on their faces had turned to lust. Intense lust.

He took hold of her arms and pulled her onto him and up to his face.

As the touching and kissing became more sensual, their ability to control their behavior broke down.

For the next hour, *Airship* rocked gently at the dock in the calm, flowing waters of the river.

Having made love for the first time, they held on tightly. Her hair draped across his face. They laughed. They kissed. They rolled over together. He climbed on top of her.

After holding and cuddling close for another hour, they made love for a second time. Out of breath, they lay back on the bed holding hands. They looked up at the overhead of the foredeck.

"Owen Flynn, you're the most exciting, loving man I've ever known. You've just driven me insane. I believe an apology is in order?"

"Okay. I'm really sorry for driving you insane. But, you drove me crazy, too. So, we're even."

"Even it is, then. I'm good with that."

She looked at her watch, "Oh my God! We need to go."

He agreed.

The two of them slid off the bed and got dressed in silence.

As they were about to leave *Airship*, Riley stopped and bent her head down,

"Oh my God. What have we done?"

29

The Crash

Riley, Viv, and Crystal met at the Dolphin.

They spent a couple of minutes laughing about a problem Crystal had with one of her clients.

They each ordered a tall Shipyard Ale and began eating the peanuts left for them by Sally, their waitress.

Riley finished her first sip of beer then leaned toward her friends, "I've been dying to tell you guys what's going on."

"Is this good news or bad?" Crystal asked.

"Both. I'll start with the good news that just might become bad news. Owen and I made love three days ago."

Viv nearly spit her peanuts out, "Jesus, Riley! Just ship me to the lab!"

Crystal fell back and spilled beer on her blouse.

Riley looked at Viv and laughed, "I wish I could ship you to the lab, but I won't."

Viv leaned forward, "Why could this possibly be bad news, for God sake?"

"Because this thing's getting way too complicated. I can't wait to see him again. And, soon. I expect my head will explode any minute now."

Crystal laughed, "Then why are you here with us? You should be naked in his arms."

"Agreed. But, this is becoming a problem. I'm lying to my husband and to my daughters about where I am and what I'm doing. I'm lying to my mother and to my sister. If any of them find out that I'm lying, I'm fucked."

Crystal continued, "How're they going to find out? Nobody knows about this except Owen and us. And, we're not going to say a word to anyone."

"I know I can trust you two, but something's going on. When I went sailing with Owen..."

Viv interrupted, "Jesus! You went sailing with him?"

"Yeah. It was awesome. I loved it. But, there was a problem. When we got back, a note was glued to my windshield. It said, *'STOP OR ELSE.'* It scared the shit out of me."

Crystal asked, "Did you see who did it?"

"No, there was nobody around. Then a week ago, all four of Owen's tires were slashed while he was at work up in Portland. He saw a green pickup truck speeding away, but he didn't get the plate number. And, just the other day somebody hacked into his computer."

Viv couldn't stay quiet, "What the fuck is going on, Riley?"

"I'm not sure who's doing this to us. Jase's been jumping out of his skin thinking I'm having an affair with Owen. Maybe it's just him. Maybe he's sent some of his crazy buddies after us. Maybe it's his family. His brothers are nasty people, too."

With her mouth wide open, Crystal jumped in again, "Ya' know something? Every now and then I've seen a green pickup truck driving by the salon. It's creepy. The guy drives by slowly looking in our front window. There was a yellow stripe across the back of it."

"Jesus, Crystal! Owen told me that the green truck he saw in his parking garage had a yellow stripe, too. Shit!"

Viv and Crystal were speechless.

Then, Viv suggested, "I've got an idea. I'm going to spend some time in town looking for that asshole to see if he drives by the salon again. If I can catch him, I'm going to follow him and find out who he is."

"That's way too risky, Viv. I appreciate your offer, but I don't trust Jase and the thugs he calls his friends."

"Riley, my love. Not to worry. I can take care of myself."

Crystal sat back, "This is so crazy. I don't know if you should do anything at all."

Riley argued, "But, Crystal, I really need to know who's watching me. Maybe this is the best way to do it. Viv'll just be out for a ride, that's all."

Viv added, "I'll stay a few cars back so he doesn't notice me. If he pulls over somewhere, I'll just turn off the road. Easy!"

Riley tried to calm Crystal down, "It sounds like Viv has experience doing this. Am I right?"

"Well, I guess you could say I do. I watch a lot of TV shows where they follow people around."

Riley took a deep breath, "God, help us. This is now becoming a reality TV show?"

The three of them ended the evening with a troubled laugh.

Two days later, Crystal pulled Riley into the breakroom, "I just saw that green truck pull up outside. He's parked almost right out our window, just one space away. Whoever's driving it didn't get out. That bastard's sitting out there in his truck just waiting for you to leave. I think you need to call Viv and let her know. She needs to do her *'follow that car'* thing."

Riley's eyes opened wide, "Show me where he is."

They walked carefully to the salon front window. Crystal casually pointed her finger just outside, one space away. The truck was facing west, away from the salon. The driver seemed to be looking out his rearview mirror.

"Yeah. That's it. It has that yellow stripe across the tailgate. I'll call Viv."

Riley went out back and called her friend, "Hi. It's me. That truck is parked just outside the salon. Can you get down here right away?"

"Actually, I was on my way to get some groceries. That can wait. I'm less than a mile from town. If I can, I'll pull into an open space in Dock Square and watch him. When he pulls out, I'll follow him."

"Okay. But, like we agreed, you have to be careful. Don't do anything stupid. I'll watch him for a bit to see if he leaves before you get here. Call me when you're parked across the street."

"Roger that," Viv said, in her best detective speak.

Two minutes later, Viv called and told Riley she was parked in the first space in Dock Square, watching the truck. She could barely see the driver and told Riley that he kept looking around.

Nothing happened for the next twenty minutes. Every now and again, Viv saw the truck driver look in her direction. She scrunched down behind the dash, but worried that the driver had noticed her looking at him and not leaving.

Suddenly, the truck started up and exited the parking space.

Crystal saw the truck leave. Then, a couple of seconds later, Viv passed by the salon in pursuit.

Crystal walked over to Riley's desk and whispered, "Viv is following the truck. Keep your fingers crossed."

"Thanks, Crystal."

Viv stayed two cars back from the truck. They crossed the Kennebunk River and proceeded on Western Avenue. When they reached the intersection at Port Road, the truck turned right and sped quickly away. The cars in front of Viv continued on without turning. When Viv turned onto Port Road there were no cars between her and the truck.

She did her best to stay with him, but she didn't want to make it obvious that she was following him. The truck pulled further away from her.

After a few turns in the road, it was clear to Viv that she'd lost the truck. He was nowhere to be seen.

"*Fuck! I really screwed up.*"

Just as she was about to stop and turn around, she looked in the rearview mirror. In disbelief, she saw the green truck heading toward her from behind. He must have found a way to circle around her.

The truck didn't slow down. Instead, it sped up and rammed the back of Viv's car. The jolt from the truck slammed her head against the headrest.

Viv screamed as she steadied to look in the rearview mirror again. In horror, she saw the truck speed up and prepare to ram her again.

"Oh, my God. What the fuck are you doing?"

She stiffened her arms against the steering wheel ready for what was coming next.

The truck hit the rear of her car again, but this time the driver had other plans. He sped up and rammed her again. Then again.

She was losing control of her car. She was terrified. She tried to look in the rearview mirror again, but her timing was off by a split second. Now at over fifty miles an hour, the truck slammed into her car. She jammed on her brakes, but it was no use. She had totally lost control.

The mysterious truck veered off just in time.

With a hard scream, Viv threw her arms in front of her face in an effort to avoid the inevitable.

Her car crashed into a huge Elm tree just ten feet off the road.

The impact had its effect. Most of the car was destroyed. Viv was pinned and unconscious in the wreckage. She didn't know it, but she was bleeding from several, major wounds. Her right lung and spleen were both seriously damaged. Her legs were broken, and her left arm was crushed.

The pickup stopped about thirty feet up the road. The driver looked through the rearview mirror to assess the results. There didn't appear to be any witnesses around who might have seen the crash.

Once satisfied that the problem was solved, the truck started moving again. Slowly at first then faster.

The driver had more work to do.

30

The Hospital

Riley had no idea what had happened to Viv.

The day went by without a single call from her.

She was desperate to find out what Viv had discovered by following the truck. She went home, eager to hear from her. She called her cell phone, but there was no answer. She called her house phone, but no one answered there either. She was more than worried.

Not long after Riley returned home, the phone rang, "Viv?"

"No, Riley, it's Crystal. I've got some horrible news."

"What is it?"

"It's Viv. I just saw a news report on TV. She's been in an accident. She's in pretty bad shape. An ambulance took her to the Medical Center up in Biddeford late this afternoon."

"Oh my God, Crystal. How bad is she? Is she going to be okay?"

"I don't know anything except what the news report said. I'm going up there right now to see her."

"Hey, wait a minute. I've got to go up there with you. I'll come by and pick you up, right away!"

After they hung up, Riley grabbed her purse and a sweater then jumped in her car. It didn't take long for her to get to Crystal's house.

She stayed outside, waiting for Riley.

When she stopped for her, Crystal jumped in.

"Jesus, Riley. What the fuck is this all about? You don't think this has anything to do with that truck?"

"I don't know. I hope they'll have some information at the hospital. Let's go."

Riley raced north to Biddeford.

Neither of them said another word all the way to the Medical Center.

After reaching the hospital, they parked, and hurried through the Emergency Room entrance.

Nearly out of breath, Riley asked the receptionist, "We're here about one of our friends who was in an accident this afternoon. Her name is Vivienne Lawler?"

Without looking up from her computer screen, the receptionist confirmed the name, "You said her name is Lawler?"

"Yes. That's correct. Vivienne Lawler. L-A-W-L-E-R."

While she scanned the records, the receptionist told Riley, "I'm pretty sure she came in a few hours ago."

In a matter of seconds, the receptionist confirmed, "Yes. We admitted a Vivienne Lawler this afternoon. She was brought in by ambulance."

Crystal joined Riley at the counter and asked, "Is she all right?"

"She's still in the ER. There's a team working on her right now."

Riley needed more answers, "Is she stable or critical or whatever you call it? Is she going to be okay?"

After putting her reading glasses back on and squinting at the computer screen again, the receptionist told Riley, "I'm sorry, but I don't have a status right now. And, I can only give out medical information to family members. I hope you understand."

Riley continued her questions, "Does your computer tell you how this happened?"

"No. But, you should be able to get that from the Kennebunkport Police. We were told they're on their way right now and will be here soon.

Can you please wait over there?" she asked, pointing to the set of chairs lined against the wall.

The two of them moved away from the reception desk. Crystal sat down. Riley was too nervous to sit. She paced the floor in tears.

Ten minutes later, a uniformed police officer walked through the emergency room entrance.

He approached the reception desk and introduced himself, "Hello. I'm Sergeant Perry from the Kennebunkport Police. I'm here to ask a patient of yours some questions. Her name is Lawler. Vivienne Lawler?"

The receptionist quickly responded, "I'm sorry, Sergeant, but Miss Lawler is still in ER. She's been badly hurt."

She pointed the officer to the two women who were asking about Viv, "Maybe those two ladies can help you. They're friends of hers."

Perry thanked the receptionist and approached Riley.

"Excuse me, miss. I'm Sergeant Perry from the Kennebunkport Police. I'm investigating an accident involving your friend. Her name is Vivienne Lawyer?"

"Yes, officer. I'm Riley Reed. This is Crystal Sands. We've been friends with Viv for a long time. How can we help you?"

He opened his note pad, "I need to ask you some questions."

"Yes, of course. We have a lot of questions for you, too."

Perry nodded his head, "First, I can tell you that her car went off the road and hit a tree at about fifty-five miles an hour. It was totaled. There were tire marks all over the road for a quarter mile leading to the tree. She wasn't wearing her seat belt. When we inspected her car, we found significant damage to the rear bumper and trunk lid. There were green paint scrapes just above her rear bumper which tells us it wasn't a car that hit her, it was probably a truck. Maybe a large pickup."

Crystal asked, "So, are you saying that someone deliberately pushed her off the road into that tree?"

The Officer looked at his note pad, "We're not really sure. The investigation probably won't be completed for a few days. So far, it looks like it was a hit and run. It could have been road rage. We haven't been able to locate anyone who saw anything. No witnesses, except for people who heard the sound of screeching tires and the crash."

Riley thought out loud, "Someone tried to kill her."

Sergeant Perry agreed, but wouldn't tell them. He continued his questions.

"Do either of you know if Miss Lawler was having a disagreement or a fight with anyone?"

Neither Riley nor or Crystal said a word. They just shook their heads.

Sergeant Perry continued to ask his questions then thanked the women and left.

"My God, Crystal. Why would anybody want to hurt Viv?"

Just then, the Emergency Room entrance opened, and Viv's husband came running through the door.

He went immediately to the reception desk to ask about his wife.

"Frank!"

He turned to Riley's voice then ran over to her, "Riley, how's Viv? What have they told you?"

"I'm so sorry, Frank. They haven't told us anything. The police were here and didn't have much to tell us either. I'm scared."

"The police found me at work about twenty minutes ago and told me what happened. They had a lot of questions, but no answers."

Riley put her arm around his shoulder and squeezed him, "We're here to help you with this. We love Viv and don't want anything to happen to her. I'm sure we'll..."

Before she finished her sentence, the double doors to the Emergency Room opened. Doctor Griffith walked into the waiting room and spoke with the receptionist, who then pointed at Frank.

Griffith crossed the room and introduced himself, "I'm Doctor Griffith. I was assisting in the ER when your wife was brought in. You are her husband?"

"Yes, I am. I'm Frank Lawler. Is my wife okay?"

Doctor Griffith looked at Riley and Crystal, "Can we have some privacy, please?"

The two of them nodded and stepped away.

The doctor continued in a soft voice "Mr. Lawler, I'm so sorry to have to tell you that your wife didn't make it. There was too much damage, and..."

"What? What do you mean she didn't make it? You mean she's dead?"

Griffith bent his head down and didn't say anything.

Frank continued, "That can't be! No!"

He began to shake and lost his balance. The doctor grabbed and steadied him, "I'm so sorry, Mr. Lawler. Believe me. We did everything we could."

As Frank tried to sit down, he sank his face into his hands and cried, "Oh, my God. Oh, my God!"

Riley and Crystal saw what was going on and feared the worst. They went over to Frank and sat on either side of him.

"What's happened, Frank?" Riley asked.

He said nothing. He continued to sob. With his face still in his hands, he just shook his head.

Crystal started to cry.

Riley's jaw fell open. She began to cry, too. She wrapped her arms around Frank and held him tight.

All three continued to hold each other as they cried together.

The world had stopped turning. All important matters disappeared. The horror took over and wouldn't let go.

Doctor Griffith tried to console Frank, "Mr. Lawler, I'm sorry, but it's going to be awhile before you can visit your wife. We have a private room for you where you can wait until I can take you to her. Would you like your wife's friends to join you?"

Frank looked through his tears at Riley and Crystal. He couldn't talk. He simply nodded agreement.

Griffith escorted the three of them down the hallway that lead to the private room.

He opened the door, entered the room, and turned on the table lamp next to the bed.

"You can press this button next to the bed and a nurse will come by to get you anything you need. Can I get you anything right now? Some water perhaps?"

Frank just shook his head. Riley and Crystal shook their heads, too. Frank laid down on the bed, still crying.

The doctor left the room and closed the door behind him.

Riley walked to the side of the bed and took hold of Frank's hand, "Oh, Frank. We are so sorry. You know we will do everything we can for you and the kids."

He turned his head and asked, "How did this happen? Why her? What am I going to tell our children? I can't live without her. I'm a dead man!"

Crystal joined Riley at the side of the bed and took Frank's other hand, "This is so incredibly horrible. I can't even imagine what you must be going through right now. But, your kids need you more now than ever. You have to be strong. You've got to be their Dad, as well as their mom, now."

Frank didn't speak. He just looked at Crystal and nodded.

The three of them turned quiet. There was nothing they could say or do that could change what had just happened.

Twenty minutes of silence went by when a knock came at the door, "Mr. Lawler, I'm nurse Holloway. May I come in?"

Riley spoke for him, "Yes, nurse, please come in."

Holloway opened the door and approached Frank, "If you're up to it, sir, you can go see your wife now. Do you need any help? I have a wheelchair out in the hall."

"No. That won't be necessary. I think I'm okay."

He got up off the bed and moved toward the door. Riley and Crystal walked behind him. The nurse helped Frank up the hall to the Emergency Room.

Doctor Griffith was waiting for them at the door, "Mr. Lawler, are you okay, sir?"

"Yes, thank you. I'm ready to see her now."

"I understand. You may feel a bit weak in there. But, you should know that when you do see her it will be as if she was sleeping peacefully."

The doctor opened the ER door, and they entered.

Viv's body lay on a gurney. A white sheet covered her from the base of her neck to her feet. There was severe damage to Viv's face. Her eyes were closed and there was no expression on her face. She was at peace.

Frank walked slowly to her side then placed his hand on hers. He could not stop crying. He didn't want to. He didn't need to.

Riley and Crystal went to the other side of the gurney where they each placed a hand on Viv's head and shoulder. Their tears were heavy with love.

No one said a word until Frank knelt down and kissed Viv's lips.

"Oh, Viv, my love. I'm so sorry. I cannot tell you...."

Frank choked up and couldn't speak.

As Riley and Crystal were saying their goodbyes to Viv, a nurse entered the ER and quietly told Doctor Griffith that Viv's three children were in the waiting room.

The doctor approached Frank, "Mr. Lawler, your children are here in the waiting room. Do you want to have them come in with you?"

"Yes, please, just for a few minutes."

As the doctor left the ER, Riley said to Frank, "Crystal and I will be leaving now so that you and your family can have some private time together. Frank, you know we love you and your children dearly and will do whatever we can to help you through this."

Frank opened his arms for Riley and Crystal to be together in his embrace, "Thank you so very much. You two were Viv's best friends, and I know this must be very difficult for you, too."

Riley and Crystal passed the children at the ER door. They all spoke briefly before they joined their father at Viv's side. The kids hugged their Dad then moved to the side of their sleeping mother.

The door closed after Riley and Crystal left. The screams of Viv's family could be heard throughout the halls of the Emergency Room.

Riley and Crystal could barely walk to the car in the parking lot. They couldn't stop crying. It wasn't simply because Viv died in an auto accident. Their brains were trying to wrestle with the real reason why Viv was now dead.

As they pulled out of the Medical Center, they didn't notice that someone across the lot had been watching for them.

31

The Gun

Three days later, Riley and Crystal attended Viv's funeral.

Jase had no interest in going and stayed home to watch a Red Sox game.

Owen wanted to go but thought it better not to.

Most of the stylists were in attendance. No one knew anything about what had happened, only that she died from a hit-and-run. The police hadn't completed their investigation into the cause of the 'accident.' But, Riley knew. And, so did Crystal.

It was a very difficult event for Riley. Losing her childhood friend while trying to help solve Riley's problem compounded her emotion. It was a struggle she'd never expected to have to endure.

She needed Owen more than ever, now.

After the funeral, Riley knew that Owen would be waiting for her on *Airship*. She drove to the yacht club and met him at the dock.

He reached out with both arms, "I'm so sorry, Honey. This has been such a horrible tragedy. We'll..."

"This should never have happened, Owen. It's all my fault. She died trying to help me. It was too dangerous. I never should have let her do it."

Owen looked into her tears, "This whole situation has become far too dangerous for us. And, now, for your friends, too. We need to protect ourselves."

Riley choked back, "I'm scared, Owen. I'm really scared. What the Hell do we do now?"

They went below and sat on the salon cushions together.

"Since the accident, I've given this a lot of thought. And, I decided how we should handle all this. Take a look in the cabinet above the sink."

Riley looked at him with a question across her face. She turned and opened the cabinet. What she saw scared her even more. It was a gun.

She didn't touch it, but instead turned back to Owen, "This is crazy. Are you suggesting we kill this guy?"

"No. That's not what we should do. I want you to be able to protect yourself, and that's what the gun is for. It'll help calm your fears."

"When did you get this?"

"I've had it for a long time. I used to go to a target range near here years ago."

"Listen, Honey. I'm scared, yes, but I'm not so sure this is going to make me feel better. I've never even held a gun in my hand before, never mind shoot someone. I don't know how to use it."

He took her in his arms, "I'll show you what to do. We'll go to the range, and I'll teach you everything you need to know."

"Christ, Honey! What the Hell has happened to us? Now I'm going to carry a gun around with me?"

"Riley, I wish we could just love each other and not be scared because we do. Your husband and his family are evil people. They're doing everything they can to stop us, but they won't. Our love for each other is too strong. But, we have to be very careful. And, you need to keep this gun close to you."

Two days later, Owen and Riley visited the gun range in Wells.

Owen got out of the car and walked around to open Riley's door. She didn't get out.

He bent down to look into her eyes, "It's not a good idea to be shooting a gun while you're sitting in a car. We need to go inside."

"I'm scared, Owen. We really need to do this?"

"I'm sorry, Honey, but the answer is 'yes.'"

Owen spent the next ninety minutes teaching Riley to safely hold the gun, load the magazine, and shoot at the target. He also showed her how to position herself and face her target with both knees bent.

After she fired off twenty rounds, he was satisfied that she knew what she was doing.

"I'm going to have some bad dreams after this."

"I understand. It happens to a lot of people who learn to shoot."

Owen pulled the target to the booth to check on Riley's accuracy.

"Well, you hit the target a few times. That's a good start. How do you feel?"

"Tired. Very tired. Can we leave now?"

"Of course. Let's go get something to eat. By the way, we'll be coming back here every few days for a while. And, I want you to keep this gun with you at all times."

"Why?"

"Because you never know if or when you might need to use it. And, I want you to be able to hit what you're aiming at."

"Fuck you!"

32

The CD

Jase went down to the basement to workout.

He hadn't spent much time at all on the exercise equipment until he discovered Riley's affair. That got him working out nearly four hours a day. That day, he planned to use the stationary bike for his cardiovascular workout.

He knew that something was going on behind his back, the cell phone logs proved it. He had enough evidence to confront Riley about the affair, but he wanted more. He had to catch her cheating on him.

He took off his tee-shirt and jeans then put on his gym clothes and sneakers. He grabbed the headphones off the shelf near the window and pulled them over his ears. Without looking at it, he picked up a CD off the home theater console and inserted it into the slot on the side of the control unit. It automatically powered on and began playing the first track into his ears.

Jase couldn't quite hear the song that began to play so he clicked the volume-up button until the only sound he heard was the music from the CD. To his surprise, it was playing *"My Sweet Lady,"* a love song by John Denver.

He stopped the bike, *"What the fuck is going on? This isn't one of our CDs."*

He hit the eject button on the player and looked it over, hoping to find some answers. There was no label on it, so someone created it.

He thought to himself, *"We don't listen to this kind of music around here."*

He pushed the CD back into the machine and poked at the play button again. He skipped ahead two, then three, tracks. Up came *"Brown Eyed Girl."* He continued listening to the rest of the disk.

He was outraged. It was nothing but love songs. He assumed that Riley had gotten them from Flynn.

His brain was boiling, *"I'm going to kill that son of a bitch. No... I'm going to kill the two of them."*

Jase downed a couple of beers and impatiently waited for his wife to come home.

After forty minutes, Riley entered the driveway and stopped at the garage, waiting for its door to finish opening.

Jase was so pissed off he couldn't wait for his wife to come in. He crashed through the kitchen screen door and ran down the steps to the driveway.

"What the fuck is going on?" he screamed at Riley through her open car window.

"Shit! What's wrong with you today?" she fired back, as she struggled to exit the car.

"I just found the fucking CD with all your love songs on it. That asshole Flynn made it for you, didn't he?"

"Goddamn you, Jase! I'm not going there. My best friend just died a few days ago, so shut the fuck up!"

"Hey, don't talk to me like that. I'm sorry that your friend is dead, but I have real problems with you and your boyfriend, Flynn."

Riley didn't respond or even look at her husband. She pushed him aside and ran past him toward the house.

He went after her, "You fucking bitch. What the Hell is going on? I've had all I can take from you and that asshole."

Before she could reach the steps to the kitchen, he grabbed the back of her blouse to slow her down. She stopped and spun around causing the back of her blouse to rip open in Jase's hand.

"You son of a bitch! Look what you just did to my blouse. Now, leave me alone."

He let go. She turned and raced up the steps, through the kitchen door then up the stairs to the bedroom. She slammed the door shut then fell on the bed crying.

He followed her and charged through the door, "You've been lying to me and the girls all this time. You better tell me the truth. And, now!"

Riley said nothing. She thought only about Viv and continued to cry.

Jase's anger at his wife was intense. He couldn't control himself any more. He picked up her right side and flipped her onto her back.

"You son of a bitch! Don't you dare touch me again!"

"I'll touch you anyway I want. You're my wife for Christ sake, and you'll stop this crap right now."

"Stop it! You're overreacting, and you're scaring me!"

His eyes were practically glowing as he grabbed her around the throat. He pushed her into the bed pillows and squeezed her larynx with both thumbs. She tried to scream, but it was impossible. He squeezed even harder. She desperately tried to pull his hands away from her neck, but he was too strong.

She was losing the battle. Her husband was strangling her, and she couldn't stop him. Any strength she had left was weakening. She couldn't breathe until finally her hands dropped to her side.

"I'm going to kill you. Then, I'm going kill him!"

Lauren came home from school and dropped her book bag on the kitchen counter. She heard her father upstairs screaming at her mother. She raced up the stairs to find Riley on the bed with her father still choking her.

She ran to the side of the bed and screamed, "Daddy! What're you doing?"

She jumped onto the bed and grabbed her father's hands in an effort to stop him, "Let go of Mom! Dad! Let go. You can't do this to her again. I don't care what she's done. You have to stop hurting her."

Jase looked at his daughter, hysterical and crying. Lauren's intervention caused Jase to loosen his hold on his wife.

Riley couldn't move. She was choking and gasping for air. She bent over the side of the bed and vomited on the floor.

Her neck was bright red from Jase's hands and fingers.

Lauren backed up against the bedroom wall and slid down to the floor, "What the Hell is going on, Dad?"

Jase crossed the room to sit in the bedroom chair. He cupped his face into his hands.

He looked up at his daughter, "I'm sorry you had to see that Lauren. I've told you and your sister before that your mother has been unfaithful to me. And, I just learned that she's still doing it. I got a little emotional. That's all."

"Dad. You almost killed her! That's not being just a little emotional."

"I really don't know how to stop her. If you or Kelly have any good ideas, let me know."

Lauren turned to her mother, "Ma. Why are you doing this to Dad? You're doing it to us, too. You need to stop it, now!"

Struggling with her speech, Riley tried to defend herself, "I'm not doing anything wrong. Your father has gone crazy. The fact that he just tried to kill me is evidence of that."

"Mom. We've told you before that Dad isn't making this stuff up. The reason he's so unhappy with you is because you're lying to him... and to us."

Lauren got up off the floor and moved to the bed.

She bent over and took her mother's hand, "I want our family to be what it used to be. I don't want you guys to ague or hurt each other anymore. I want us all to be happy again. If you're cheating on Dad, you need to stop it immediately. And, you have to tell us the truth. So, are you seeing this guy? Really?"

Riley looked her daughter in the eyes and lied to her, "Absolutely not. I'm not seeing him or anybody else. Like I said, your father's making this up. It's all in his imagination."

Lauren didn't say anything to her mother. She just stared at her.

She knew her Mom was lying again.

33

The Keys

A week later, Owen and Julie went into town to do some shopping.

For years, they had enjoyed spending hours in downtown Kennebunkport. They would browse through the Candy Man, Compliments, Whimsy, The Good Earth, and all the other great shops in town. They made time to stop at Ben & Jerry's for some ice cream.

One of their favorite shops was Abacus, just across Dock Square from Compliments Gallery. The great thing about Abacus was the variety of cute and wonderful treasures to be found as they searched for goodies to take home.

They split up on their own.

Julie went off and stopped to consider buying an ornate table clock. She decided not to get it. Nevertheless, Julie continued her search.

Owen walked through the shop and examined several items through their glass cases. He descended the few steps at the back of the shop. As he browsed around, he found two baskets on the counter that attracted his attention. The first was a collection of silvery 'Love Tokens,' each with its own message for lovers. He found one that said 'Love forever.' Another said 'I'm yours.'

But, next to the Love Tokens was a basket full of miniature skeleton keys, each unique from the others. His thoughts of Riley were overwhelming.

He liked the Love Tokens, but a stronger thought entered his mind, *"The key to my heart."*

He looked back to ensure he was still out of sight from his wife, selected two keys, and quickly paid for them with his credit card. He took the keys out of the bag and pushed them into his jeans pocket. He looked around for a waste basket but couldn't find one. So, he crinkled the bag with the receipt still in it then stuffed it into his sweatshirt pocket.

He rejoined Julie to continue their shopping together.

"Did you find anything good back there?"

He looked over his shoulder to the back of the store, "They had some really interesting things, but nothing we can't do without."

"I bought a cute little sign for the kitchen."

She showed it to him, *"Many have eaten here. Few have died."*

"I like that. Where do you want to put it?"

"Not sure, yet. Certainly, somewhere on the kitchen wall. We'll see when we get home."

The two spent another hour wandering around the Dock Square shops.

They stopped for lunch at Alisson's. Even though they knew everything that was in it, they looked through the menu. She ordered the Clam Strips, and he got the Lobster Mac and Cheese.

After a few awkward moments, Julie put her elbows on the table and asked, "What's wrong, Owen?"

"What do you mean? Nothing's wrong that I know of."

"That's bullshit, and you do know it. Tell me what's going on."

Before he responded, he knew he had to either tell her the truth or lie once again. He hated having to lie to his wife. Either way, it was going to be a bad answer.

He wasn't really sure yet where his love for Riley was going. Was it going to resolve itself into divorce from Julie? Will Riley divorce Jase? Will their problems finally force her to give up and return to her family? He was faced with so many unanswered questions.

He decided to lie to Julie again, "Nothing's going on. I've just been busy at work. There are a lot of problems at the airport, and they're counting on me to fix them. That's all."

Julie leaned forward, "No. I'm not talking about your job. I'm talking about us. Do you still love me?"

"Love you? Sure, I do. It's just different than it was."

"Like what? How's it different?"

He paused then explained, "Julie, when we first got married, everything was exciting. We were so passionate and intimate back then. It's all so different now."

"Does that mean you don't love me anymore?"

He tried to console her, "We have so many different interests now. We have communication problems that confuse me. I don't understand you sometimes. I'll get over it. Trust me."

They went back home. Zeke had waited patiently for them and ran over to Owen when he came through the door. He anticipated a good belly scratching from his 'Dad.'

After a few minutes with his buddy, Owen headed to the bathroom.

Still in the kitchen, Julie noticed a bulge in Owen's sweatshirt pocket. He had draped it over the back of one of the kitchen chairs. She picked it up and pulled a crumpled, brown, paper bag out of the pocket. Her curiosity had the best of her. She opened the top of the bag and looked inside. She found a receipt from Abacus. Nothing else. She read the details of the transaction. It listed two silver keys. She searched deeper into the bag, but there was nothing there. She checked around the kitchen table and floor but found nothing.

"What's going on here?" she asked herself.

When Owen returned to the kitchen, she was holding the bag and the receipt in her hands.

Fearing she already knew the answer, she asked, "What's this?"

He looked at her then at the bag and the receipt. His first thought was, "*Fuck! What do I do now?*"

He had to stay cool, "I bought something to surprise you. I was going to find a special moment to give this to you. I guess there's no time like the present."

He dug into his jeans' pocket and pulled out the two keys. He opened his hand to show her.

"So, you're going to tell me that these keys were for me?"

"Actually, there's one for you and one for me. One's the key to my heart and the other is the key to yours."

She couldn't contain her anger, "Do you really think I'm an idiot? Really? These aren't for you and me. They're for you and your girlfriend."

He tried to calm her down, "That's absurd. I don't have a girlfriend. I have a wife, and these keys are meant for us. That's the truth."

Before Julie ran out of the kitchen, she screamed at him, "You're a lying son of a bitch. I want you to stop and think. Do you want her or do you want me?

You can't have both."

34

The Ultimatum

Riley arrived home from work.

But, before she got out of her car, she sat looking at the garage door.

She asked herself, *"What's going on? Someone kills my best friend? This has got to be about Owen and me! I just know it. So, now, someone's out to hurt us any way they can."*

She continued to sit in the car, pondering the many things that were going wrong for them. She decided to put all those thoughts away for another time and go into the house.

She got out of the car and was about halfway up the porch stairs when she was confronted by Lauren who'd been waiting for her to come home.

"Hi, Kiddo. How was school today?"

"I haven't any idea how school was today. I spent most of my time pissed off at my mother."

"Why are you pissed at me? What've I done to hurt you?"

She walked past her daughter and into the kitchen. Lauren turned and followed right behind her. Her face was wrinkled from the anger she felt.

With a screech in her voice, Lauren yelled, "I've had it with you, Mom. This stuff I've heard from Dad is now all over school. You're hurting all of us with this thing you're doing behind our backs. You have to stop it before it gets worse."

While Lauren continued the outrage with her mother, Kelly came down from her room and joined in, "What's going on? I can't do anything up there with all the screaming. What happened?"

To prevent her mother from answering her sister's question, Lauren jumped in front of Riley and responded, "You know all this shit that's been going on with Mom. Remember Dad told us about the affair she's having? Well, the news is all over town and in school, too. Kids are laughing at us and talking behind my back. I'm bullshit, and I want Mom to stop what she's doing."

Riley tried to calm her down, "Lauren, sweetheart, nothing's going on. A small town like ours always has a rumor mill. Most of the stuff you hear are just lies or misunderstandings. Does anyone have any evidence that I'm having an affair? The answer is *'no'* because none of it is true."

Before she left the kitchen, Kelly went after her mother, screaming, "You're lying! Just like Dad said. You're lying! You need to be honest with us. Too many people are talking about you and that Flynn guy. What is wrong with you? We've been a good and happy family. Look at this incredible home we have. Dad is the best Dad we could ever want. How about us, your daughters? And, Dad told us this guy's an asshole. What the fuck? You're just sick! You're very, very sick, Ma!"

Kelly burst into tears as she ran out of the kitchen.

After Kelly left, both Riley and Lauren were quiet. Neither wanted to talk. It was an awkward silence. They didn't even look at each other.

Riley decided that something needed to be said, "Well, I guess we've heard how Kelly feels, and..."

Lauren stopped her, "Mom, that's how I feel, too. And, that's how Dad feels. Don't you know you're destroying our family? Don't you even care about us?"

"Of course, I care. I told you there's nothing going on. This all started with your Aunt Ella. She saw a man come into the salon, and she dreamed up this crazy idea that there was something going on between us. It's not true, for God sake."

Lauren raised her voice, "Oh, really? Aunt Ella showed us phone records of calls between you and Flynn. There's no way that he's just a client of yours. You can't deny it's happening."

Riley attempted to change the subject, "Look, Lauren. I think you and I need some time together so we can talk. How about if we go shopping tomorrow?"

"Bullshit, Mom! That's not going to work. This is very serious. I can't continue to be your daughter if you're going to destroy our home. Either it's Flynn or it's me. Make your choice, now! It's either him or me!"

"I love you. And, I love your sister. We need to stay together and be happy just like we've always been. I would never hurt you. You must believe me."

"Okay. But, like I said, who's it going to be Ma? I asked you to make your choice. And, right now! Him or me?"

"I told you I love you. You cannot give me an ultimatum. I won't allow it. Not for me, your father, or our family. Everyone just needs to settle down and get over this nonsense."

Riley left the kitchen unhappy with herself for fabricating yet more lies.

35

The Breakup

The next day, Julie had been up most of the night.

She decided it was time to confront her husband about his affair. She spent time in the bathroom just staring into the sink and thought about what she was going to say to him.

Finally, she got up the courage, left the bathroom, and went down to the kitchen.

Owen was relaxing at the table, drinking his second cup of coffee, and reading his Boston Globe.

"Owen, we need to talk."

"Oh? What's it about, this time?"

"It's about you and that bitch, Riley Reed. I've had it with you. I can't go through this any longer. I just want to kill the two of you."

He laid the newspaper on the table and focused on his wife, "Look, sweetheart. I made a mistake. I'm sorry for putting you through all this."

"But, you keep seeing her. Don't you think I know? Don't you know I can tell when you're lying?"

He took a deep breath, "Look, I don't want to hurt our marriage any longer. How can I prove it to you?"

She looked him straight in the eye and poked his chest with her finger, "Okay, then. Here's the deal. You go tell her it's over. Then come right back home. If you're really serious, you'll end it with her and join me for a weekend away from here. I'll even go out on that damn boat of yours, for

God sake! But, if you don't end it with her now, then it's all over. I'll divorce you, put you out on the street, and take everything you have!"

He hung his head, "Like I said, I'm sorry for putting you through all this. I really am. I need to take Zeke for a walk. I won't be long. We'll talk some more when we get back."

She stared at him as he silently attached Zeke to his leash and headed out back.

She made her final point as he closed the screen door, "It'd better be a short walk. My patience with you is all used up."

She went into the living room to wait for him. Her arms were folded in front of her as she began to cry.

Owen and Zeke walked across the lawn and wound their way through the rocks to the narrow beach below. As usual, Zeke wanted off the leash, and Owen submitted.

The rocky coast of Maine was persistent. The beach on which they attempted to walk was littered with rocks of all shapes and sizes. It was low tide, so the waves were shallow. The small, sandy beach was exposed, making it a little easier to walk.

Zeke ran after four gulls. Owen walked through the wetness of the waves. He located his favorite rock and sat to watch his dog chase the birds across the wet sand. The water was cold, but Zeke didn't mind.

The time he spent with Zeke offered him solace and a place to contemplate Julie's demand. He looked across the water. The sky was bright blue with only a hint of clouds. A half-dozen Sandpipers scrambled across the beach looking for their breakfast. Two sailboats passed offshore heading against the wind. They appeared to be racing one another. He smiled at the thought.

But, he couldn't think of the water, the sky, and sailing any longer. He needed to think seriously about Riley and the problems he'd created.

He realized he had few options. None of them had good outcomes. He loved Riley more deeply than Julie. He was certain of it. But, he'd been married to his wife for a long time. They had three children together who'd be heartbroken if he left their mother. What about Riley's two daughters? They'd be deeply hurt, too, if their mother left them.

"What am I doing? Riley and I are thinking only of ourselves. She has a family who love her dearly. They'd be devastated if we continued this. I'm hurting Julie badly, too."

The only real option was to end the affair with Riley. He needed to tell her that it was over, and he needed to tell her as soon as possible.

Owen returned to the kitchen. His wife was sitting at the table with her head in her hands, crying. She was convinced that Owen was going to leave her. The agony was intense.

Owen sat next to her, "I need to go and tell her that it's over. I need to tell her that I've decided to stay with you."

Julie looked up at him in disbelief, "Don't lie to me, Owen. This has been desperately painful for me. If this is what you want, then it must be the only option. You'll never see her again. You must promise me that."

"I promise you that it's over. I'm going to go and see her. I'm going to tell her that she must go back to her family. And, that I'm going back to mine."

Julie said nothing as Owen walked out to the garage and into his car.

Riley was on her way to the salon when her private phone began to vibrate.

It was Owen, "Hey honey! What's up?"

He was careful to respond, "I can't talk now. Can we meet right away?"

Riley heard a strain in his voice, "Is there something wrong?"

"I have to go. Please get up to Biddeford. I'll tell you then."

He hung up. Riley looked at her phone as the call shut down. She started to worry.

She found an open parking lot where she could turn around.

Riley was terrified by his call. She was worried, too, that Jase might call the salon looking for her. If one of the girls told him she'd not been in yet, he would surely suspect she was meeting with Owen. And, he'd be right.

She called the salon. The phone system announced that it was Riley calling.

Dotty picked up the phone, "Good morning, Riley. How are you?"

"Hi, Dotty. I'm fine thanks. I'll be a little delayed this morning. I have to pick up some product I ordered at the supplier in Biddeford. I'll be back at the salon in about an hour and a half."

"No problem, Hon'. Everything's fine, here. Take your time."

After saying goodbye, Riley hung up and told herself, *"Lying to my friends really sucks, too!"*

Riley made her way to Biddeford. When she arrived, Owen was already parked in his usual spot. She pulled in next to him and noticed that he wasn't smiling when he saw her.

Riley feared the worst.

Owen went around the back of her car to the front door. He opened it and bent down so he would be able to talk with her face-to-face.

He spoke first, "Hi. You okay? You look a little stressed out."

"Yeah, I guess I'm a little stressed. It's that damn call of yours. What's wrong?"

Owen's eyes turned toward the front of her car, "Yeah. I'm a little stressed, too."

She pushed her left hand out to Owen in an offer to hold hands, "Tell me what's happened."

He took her hand and returned his eyes back to hers, "I've been very bothered lately about us. This relationship of ours is tearing your family apart. They're hurt, and they're angry. Especially Kelly and Lauren. And, your..."

"It's troubling to me, too. As for Kelly, she's hated me from birth. I don't know why, but it's true. And, Lauren's just too young to get her head around any of this. Every time I go out she cries now. I've thought about this every night, but there's nothing we can do about it. As for Jase, I don't really give a shit about him."

"Are you saying you don't love him now because of me?"

She dropped her head for a moment then looked deep into his eyes, "I never knew what true happiness was until I met you. I thought I loved Jase, too, but I was wrong. You've made me incredibly happy. I feel safe with you. I feel strong with you. I feel at peace with you. I..."

Owen stopped her, "But, Honey, what you're telling me is that I really am the problem here. If it weren't for me, you'd be at home with your family spending the rest of your life with them. Loving them as they need your love. Can't you see? Their hatred of me is justified. Christ, you should hate me, too, for doing this to you. And, to them."

She couldn't believe what she was hearing, "So, what are you telling me? Are you saying this is over for us?"

"It has to be."

"That's just crazy, Honey. Why?"

"It's because I'm in your way. You can't be unhappy with them because you're happy with me. Don't you see it?"

"But, I need to be with you. I don't care about Jase, and, in time, my girls will understand. I can't go back to him."

"Then you need to divorce him. Throw him out of the house. Then, put your arms around your girls and tell them that he's the problem, not you."

"Okay. But, why do we have to stop seeing each other?"

"Because I'm not the man for you. Somewhere out there is a man looking for you. His name is Frank, or Tom, or Charlie. Yeah, Charlie. And, he'll be much younger than I am. He'll be taller, healthier, and smarter. He'll be really handsome, and he'll be making so much money you'll never have to work again for the rest of your life."

Through her tears, she fought back, "I could never love another man as much as I love you. If we do break this off, I won't stop. I can't stop. I need you, Owen."

"But, we have to stop. You must go back to your family."

"Owen, is this about Julie? She really is the woman you've been looking for all your life. Isn't she?"

"Honey, you're wrong. Let me just ask you this, is it possible for a man to love a woman so much that he has to leave her to make her happy? The answer is *'Yes.'* And that's what this is all about."

Her crying turned uncontrollable, "You'll see, too, that we must stay together. If you really love me then this won't end."

"I do love you. And, that's the problem. I have to leave, now."

He kissed her one last time then closed her door. They both cried as she whispered "1-4-3" at him through her window. She started her car, hesitated for a moment then pulled out. In a few seconds, she was back on Route 1 speeding toward Kennebunkport.

He didn't move. He just stood there looking at the ground where her car had been. His heart was torn open. His tears continued as it started to rain again.

Julie was at the kitchen table nervously waiting for her husband to return. Since he'd left two hours earlier, she'd been in and out of tears the whole time.

She'd gone over her questions at least ten times, *"What will I do if he really wants to end our marriage? Will he move out? Will I? What will our kids say? What will our friends think? Who will help me get through all this? What if he does end it with Riley? Can I really trust him again? Can I ever believe him again? Will I survive this?"*

She spun the questions through her head so much that twice she vomited into the sink.

Julie saw Owen pull up in front of the house, not the back. So, she was resigned to the probability that he was going to leave her. She buckled over in pain, ran up to the bedroom, and laid on the bed.

Owen went in and walked down the hallway to an empty kitchen, "Sweetheart. Where are you?"

At first, she was afraid to respond. He called her again.

"I'm upstairs."

Slowly he walked up to the bedroom. Julie continued to cry. He sat next to her and rubbed her shoulders.

He bent down to her ear and whispered, "I want to put our life back together."

She hesitated then turned onto her back.

She stared long and hard at him looking for a lie, "Are you saying that it's over with her? Just like that you ended it? How's that possible?"

"Yes. I explained to her that I've come to see just how wrong I've been. That we've both been wrong. I told her about the problems we've caused and the hurt we've inflicted on everyone. It just had to stop, and now."

Still doubtful, Julie put her arms around him. He put his around her. They held each other tight. She couldn't control her crying again, but for a different reason. He pulled his arms tight around her as Zeke waddled into the bedroom wagging his tail.

After they discussed more about his talk with Riley, they packed a suitcase for three days. With Zeke on his leash and food and supplies from the kitchen, they left for *Airship*.

36

The Pain

While Riley drove back to Kennebunkport, she could barely see the road.

Her tears would not stop. She couldn't believe that Owen had just ended their affair. And, he did it in less than three minutes. There was no discussion. She barely got in a word. There was no way for her to object to what he was telling her. He left her in shock and very pissed off. Yes, their love was a big gamble, but she believed they could still make it work.

Her mind spun a web of questions, *"What have I done wrong? I've loved this man for a year now. I haven't asked anything of him except that he love me as much as I loved him. Or, is it possible that he just doesn't really love me at all? Has he been lying to me all along?"*

She drove on as best she could. As she got closer to her salon she started to stress out about Jase.

She worried, *"What if he tried calling me at the salon while I was with Owen? Is he going to ask me where I've been? I have to make something up that he'll believe. But, I'm not really a good liar. Maybe I should just tell him the truth? But, I think, though, that this will never end."*

Riley entered the salon and Sammy looked up from her client, "Jase's been looking for you. He said he needed to talk with you right away. He's not in a good mood, so watch out."

"Thanks, Sammy. I'll go call him back."

Riley went out back to call Jase. She hesitated at first. He was the last person she wanted to talk to. Her mood was somber. Her eyes welled up when she thought about Owen breaking up with her. Life seemed to have come to a screeching halt.

Jase answered her call, "Where the fuck have you been? Were you off with that asshole, Flynn?"

"I had to go up to Biddeford to get some... Ah. No, Jase. I won't lie to you anymore. Listen. You're right. I was with him. But, we talked about the trouble we've caused everyone. We ended it today."

"Bullshit, Riley. Do you expect me to believe you? You've got balls lying to me again! I don't believe you one bit."

"I understand why you don't believe me, but it's true. Owen and I are not going to see each other anymore. It's over. He wants me to make up with you and the girls so we can have a good and happy family again."

"And, what do you want, Riley?"

Being careful with her words, "I want everyone to be happy. And, I don't want to lie anymore."

"Impossible! I don't believe you. Not for a second. You've cheated on me for a long time, now. How can I trust you ever again?"

"I can't prove it to you. You'll just have to believe me."

He was furious, "You want me to just believe you? Is that it? For years, my mother's been telling me to watch out with you. Her senses told her that you'd cheat on me someday. And, she was right. You make me sick. And, I'm telling you now, I'm going to strangle that bastard to be sure you don't cheat on me again."

"Well, that's absurd, and you know it."

"Not at all, Riley. I swear to you, if he ever comes within fifty feet of you he's a dead man. Do you understand me?"

Riley nodded into the phone, "Yeah. I understand. I'll see you at home, and we can talk more, then."

Neither said goodbye as they hung up together.

She told herself, *"I'm not married to just any asshole. I'm married to a very sick asshole."*

Riley returned to her desk to prepare for Joan Carter, her only client of the day. Thank God for that. How was she going to get through this?

Her head was spinning. Her love for Owen was so complete.

She still couldn't believe what had just happened, *"Is Owen really telling me the truth, or is he just not in love with me anymore? Is he seeing someone else? He can't be serious about restoring his marriage to Julie. It's beyond repair, just like my marriage to Jase. It's just not possible to end this, and he knows that."*

She couldn't talk. She was as quiet as she'd ever been in her life. Of course, Joan just loved to talk, but was getting no reaction from Riley at all.

Joan bent her head down to look up into Riley's sad eyes, "Hey. You okay?"

"Yeah. I'm sorry. I've just got a lot on my mind today. So, you said that you and your husband went to the Grand Canyon?"

For the last twenty minutes of the manicure, they had a conversation. Not an interesting one, but a conversation, nonetheless.

When the manicure was finished, Joan remained at Riley's desk while the nail polish dried. Riley used the time to quickly clean up around her desk. She went back to the breakroom and put on her rain coat.

Back at the desk, it was obvious to Joan that Riley was in a hurry, "Hey! I need to give you a check for my manicure."

"That's all right, Joan. This one's on the house. Have a good night."

As Riley headed for the front door, Joan called out, "Hey, thanks Riley! I hope you feel better."

Riley called back over her shoulder, "Yeah, me, too. Thanks!"

She left the salon and said goodnight to each of the stylists as she quickly passed them on her way out the door.

Most of her team felt that Riley was really pissed off about something.

Each hoped it wasn't them.

37

The Trail

A week went by, and Riley was still in tears over the breakup with Owen.

She hadn't slept at all. She spent every available minute on her treadmill. She only played with her food. Everywhere she looked she saw his eyes. They haunted her. They consumed her.

She was certain that the breakup wouldn't last. She expected that Owen would call her any minute. But, the phone didn't ring.

She asked herself again, "*What's he doing right now? Is he at work up at the airport? Is he out on Airship? Does he think of me the way I can't stop thinking about him? Does he really love me, and is he in pain like I am? Is he really working on restoring his marriage to Julie or was that a lie?*"

She decided that she needed to see him in person so she could ask him her questions, and more. She tried calling him on his special phone, but he didn't answer. For three days she tried calling, but she got the same result. Nothing.

Frustrated, she took off from the salon one afternoon and drove to the airport in Portland. She knew where he parked his car so she pulled up behind it.

When she saw his *"Combat Wounded"* license plate, *"CHOPR,"* her tears began to fall again. She had an immediate flashback to the times they spent in his car and on his boat loving each other. She felt the hugs, the kisses, the intimacy, and the laughter they shared.

She convinced herself that he wanted to see her. But, how? She believed, too, that it would have to be when they were both out driving on the road.

Owen's workday was coming to an end, so she decided to hide along his route home. She'd follow him in the hopes that he'd see her and pull into their secret spot in Biddeford.

About a mile from the airport, Riley found a convenient place to stop with sufficient foliage to hide most of her car. It also gave her a good view of who was coming down the road.

She waited. After nearly an hour, her frustration had become painful. Owen was nowhere to be seen. Still, she waited.

Finally, she spied his Jeep coming toward her. She ducked down in her seat to disappear below the car door. He passed her.

She straightened up in her seat, started the engine, and checked to see if any traffic was coming. Damn! It being rush hour, there were about ten cars coming down the road with no openings between them. She had to wait for all of them to pass.

She lost sight of Owen's car. She had no options. She had to maintain her place in the convoy in front of her.

But, up ahead was the Biddeford Shopping Center parking lot. She was sure he'd be waiting for her there.

She pulled off the road into the lot then raced around the corner to their favorite spot behind Planet Fitness.

But, he wasn't there.

Pissed at him for not stopping at their special hideout, she headed home. But, along the way she decided to drive past his house. She hoped that he'd be out where she might see him, or he might see her.

As she approached his driveway, she slowed. She didn't want to alert anyone so she casually glanced out the driver-side window. Nothing. He wasn't out there.

"Damn you, Owen Flynn! I'll not let you get away from me! I'll be back..."

She sped up and turned south on Shore Road toward home.

Along the way, she devised another plan.

38

The Vigil

Riley's frustration with Owen was off the charts.

She needed to find a way to connect with him. She had to find a way to get him alone.

Then, it dawned on her, "*Airship! He's sure to be alone on his boat.*"

The next day was Saturday, and he'd likely be at his boat early in the morning. She decided to get to the yacht club well before he arrived.

Riley got up at 5:30, well before Jase. She quietly got dressed and went to the kitchen to make coffee, expecting to give a cup to Owen. She packed a basket with two coffees, some French pastry, juice, and all the ingredients for a wonderful, dawn breakfast on the boat.

She quietly pulled out of the driveway and onto the road toward town. She steered around Dock Square and onto Ocean Avenue. In less than a minute she pulled into the Arundel Yacht Club parking lot and found a good place to wait for him.

She waited. It was 6:20, and he hadn't arrived yet. She waited some more.

At 7:05, Owen pulled into the lot and parked in his special spot.

Riley's heart began to pound. Being so close now was even more exciting than she'd imagined it would be. They'd not spoken to one another for nearly a month and a half now, and it had become unbearable. She finally had the opportunity to resolve his problems with her and their relationship.

She waited for him to get out of his car before she approached him. There. The car door opened, and he got out. Riley started to open her door, when Owen's passenger door opened. Julie got out of the car.

"What the fuck! You bitch," Riley screamed to herself.

She slunk in her seat to avoid being seen. She peered over the dashboard at him as he walked to his trunk. He opened the cargo door and pulled out his sailing gear and bags. It was obvious that he and Julie were going to spend some time on *Airship*.

Julie joined him at the back and pulled out a small cooler.

They were smiling at each other as they started their walk to the dock.

Riley couldn't believe what she had just seen. Owen and Julie were happy together. They looked to be in love as they boarded *Airship*.

In her mind, she asked him, *"What the Hell are you doing? Airship is our boat, not hers. You can't do this to me!"*

She started to cry, again. At first, a tear fell from each eye then it became a flood. The pain of losing him forever was more than she could take. And, seeing him happy with his wife was unbearable.

Her mind was full of wild ideas. She considered going onto *Airship* to confront the two of them. But, she decided that would be a mistake. She had to be patient. She believed that she would get him alone one day, and soon.

She watched as the two of them rigged the boat for sailing and departed the yacht club dock. She was furious to see Julie with her arm around his shoulder as he steered *Airship* out onto the river.

"Oh my God, Owen! I'm dying here. I think only of you. All day and all night. I miss you so much. I need you. I want you. I love you…

Yet, you just forgot about me with the snap of your fingers? I am sick. I can't smile anymore. I hurt so much. I can't get over you, nor do I want to.

Please, Owen, call me and tell me you love me, too. Call me!"

39

The Pursuit

It had been another week, and Riley's agony had not worn off.

Her determination to get to Owen was stronger than ever. Her love for him was stronger, too. She'd never felt this way before about anyone. Never.

She planned to follow him, again, in the hopes that he'd change his mind. If he saw her, he was bound to want to meet with her.

Or, so she thought.

Riley got ready to go to work and said goodbye to Jase. It was just after 8:00 when she pulled out of the garage and turned onto North Street toward town. But, instead of continuing to her salon, she turned at Dock Square and headed away from town.

Her heart beat faster as she approached Windemere. When she entered his street, she slowed and watched for him. She passed his house but saw no activity.

At the corner of Windemere and Seaview, she pulled off the road, shut off her engine, and concentrated her eyes in the rearview mirror.

Nothing. She waited. Again, nothing.

An hour and ten minutes went by, and she was about to give up when she saw his car exiting his driveway. He was on his way to Portland and would be late for work.

As he turned north on Shore Road, she slowly moved in behind him. By then, he was a quarter of a mile ahead of her.

She planned to stay far enough back so he didn't notice her just yet. She was both excited and anxious but didn't want to upset him.

She thought about what she was going to say to him once he recognized her car and pulled over, *"Do I just want him to answer my questions? Do I want to tell him how much I love and miss him? Does he want us to get back together?"*

So many questions yet to be answered.

There was no traffic, so she sped up a bit to get a little closer to him.

Her heart was going wild. She stared at him ahead of her. She decided that she was going to tell him that she loved him more than ever and wanted their affair to continue.

She got closer. Any minute and he would surely realize she was behind him.

But, he didn't stop. In fact, he sped up. It was apparent that he had recognized her car and wasn't going to pull over.

She was frustrated beyond belief. He wasn't stopping. It was a horrid reality that he didn't want to talk to her.

She stayed close to him all the way to the airport garage. He parked in his usual spot. Then, she pulled up behind him. She got out of her car and walked up to his door as he was getting out.

She pointed back toward the road and screamed, "Why didn't you stop when you saw it was me back there? Didn't you realize I need to talk with you?"

After closing and locking his car door, he turned to her, "Look, Riley. I thought we had an understanding?"

"Understanding? Is that what's happened to us? Our love has become an understanding?"

"I told you that I was in your way. I was the problem. Your family needs you. You all need to be happy again, and I was keeping you from it."

"I can't just turn off my love for you. Maybe you can, but I can't!"

Owen stared at her, "Do you think I just turned you off like a light switch? My love for you was, and still is, complete. I have no room left in my heart except for you. But, that's wrong. Your family wants me dead because I somehow stole you away from your husband. I'm twenty-five years older than you, for Christ sake. What magic spell did I cast over you that pulled you away from your family? Jesus!"

"You know that's crazy. I love you for the man you are. It wouldn't matter to me if you were a hundred years older. You make me happy. You make me feel loved. You treat me like a woman. You trust and respect me for who I am. I will never get that from Jase. Never!"

He was careful to find the right words, "Honey, we can't do this. As much as I want us to continue, we can't. It's tearing your family apart. And, that's wrong."

"I saw you at the yacht club weeks ago. You were with Julie. You looked happy together. Is this really about her?"

"I need to repair my marriage just like you need to repair yours. This has been a big mistake..."

"Mistake? Our love is a mistake? You son of a..."

"No. I didn't mean that. What I meant was that our love has hurt other people. And, badly. Your daughters are an emotional wreck. Your husband wants to kill not just me, but the both of us. I've been trying to keep my marriage together, but it's been very difficult. Julie doesn't trust me at all."

"The other day I asked Jase if we could have an open relationship where he would allow our affair to continue, and I would still be married to him."

Owen snapped back against his car, "Open relationship? I can't imagine him allowing that. Besides, I couldn't share you with him. Not for a minute."

"Well, don't worry. I thought he was going to strangle me again. Only this time for good."

"I'm sorry. But, we shouldn't be together. We shouldn't be talking. Like I said, we have to end this. Please let me go. I have to get out of your way."

He bent toward her and kissed her on the cheek. After he straightened up, with his head hung down, he turned and started to walk toward his office.

"Owen, please don't walk away. This is not over. We will be together. You'll see."

40

The Gloom

For the next few months, Riley did her best to rebuild her marriage with Jase.

But, he still didn't trust her. His need to control her behavior had become intolerable. He questioned her whereabouts any time she was out of the house. He continued to accuse her of flirting with other men. Only, it became much worse.

She was compelled to be submissive. If she strayed even the slightest from Jase's rules and demands, she spent most of her time at home being verbally and physically abused. Her daughters and his family were on his side and spied on her all the time. They reported even the slightest deviation to Jase, resulting in more screaming.

Riley was trapped in a ten-room cage and couldn't escape. She was allowed to go to work or the grocery store then back home immediately. She was required to report her activities in detail and identify the exact time when she was in one place or another.

No one believed her. She saw no positive end to her problems at all.

But, her love for Owen continued to grow. Her need to run into him was all she could think about. She couldn't resist the urge to follow him in the hopes that he still loved her and would give in.

As he went about life without her, every now and then Owen recognized Riley's car. He found it odd that she seemed to be wherever he was.

He returned home from work one evening and found Julie at the kitchen table eager to confront him, "So. I saw your old girlfriend following you through town today."

"My old girlfriend?"

"You know who I mean. Riley Reed's been following you around town. Don't tell me you didn't know."

He searched for the right words to respond, "When I'm driving, I don't spend any time looking around to see if anyone's following me. What makes you think she's doing that?"

"Don't pretend you don't know. I've followed her, and she's out there looking for you all the time."

"So, you're following her now? This is getting crazy. Why?"

"I want to see what she's up to and where she's going. I hate all this, Owen. This is not what I want in my life.

"Look. This has got to be a coincidence. She can't be following me. That's just your imagination running wild."

"Not at all. I know women better than you do. Believe me. She's following you."

He tried to explain to Julie again, "I made it very clear to her that we needed to stop seeing each other. I told her to go back to her family. She needs to leave us alone."

On the outside, he appeared to be serious about his commitment to end his affair. But, inside was a different story. It was a longing. It was emotional pain. It was sensual starvation. It was a never-ending dream. He wanted Riley. He needed her. He loved her.

But, he had to keep these feelings hidden from Julie and from everyone else. Especially from Riley. He had to pretend that his marriage was on the mend and that he was happy in his life with Julie.

But, Riley kept haunting him. He struggled with the spell she had over him, but his love for her would not let go.

Week after week, he saw her in town. He kept running into, then away, from her. He tried to avoid her by using different streets and routes in and out of town. But, she found them all.

One day, while waiting at a stop light, she pulled up next to him and slid down her window.

"Hey, handsome. I see we finally meet again. Do you have time to...?"

The light turned green and interrupted her. He waved goodbye as he drove away.

Riley was devastated. The man she loved so deeply had just sped off, avoiding her. This was just the opposite of what she'd hoped from him. If he really loved her, as he said he did, he would have taken the time to talk with her.

But, no. He was gone. He just took off.

Three more months went by.

Riley spent her time distressed over both the way her family was treating her and her unrequited love for Owen. She dreamt about being with him nearly every night. Every dream she had involved the two of them making love together on *Airship*. She walked for miles on her treadmill listening to love songs that reminded her of him. She read romance novels and cried incessantly. She rarely ate a whole meal and, as such, lost more weight than she should have.

And, whenever she could get away with it, she tried to find him so that she could follow him around.

She changed her hair color and her hair style. She traded in her car for a different make, model, and color. She changed her car registration. She scheduled her appointments so she could be on the road when he was coming from or going to work. She was doing everything she could to be clever about finding him.

But, no matter how much she followed him around, she was not getting him back. Her frustration was agonizing.

Her relationship with Jase and her daughters was nearly at an end. She didn't sleep in the same room with Jase anymore. She didn't make dinners for him or for the girls. She didn't do their dishes or their laundry. She just went to work, came home, and went to bed.

Jase's attempts to reconcile their marriage were having no impact at all. He managed to get her to attend couples' therapy sessions with a marriage counselor. But, she rarely said a word.

Life for the Reed family had become a nightmare. None of them smiled at, or laughed with, one another. Riley was sad all the time. T

They all sensed that the marriage was doomed.

41

The Bottle-Return

It was a sunny, but cold winter day.

Owen was off doing errands around town. He filled up his car at Warren's, stopped at the tailor shop to pick up his repaired winter coat, and parked at the super market to return the bottles and cans that had accumulated in the basement for the past two weeks.

He went into the store and stopped to retrieve a shopping cart. As he was putting the bags of returnables in the cart, he looked up through the store's front window and saw Riley walking toward the entrance.

For over a year now, he'd tried very hard to avoid running into her. He knew she'd been following him around town. He had been looking for her, too. He was still madly in love with her, and it had been painful to stay out of her way.

But, then, there she was walking toward him. He thought to himself, *"She's more beautiful than ever."* He couldn't help but notice that she was thinner. Her smile was the same, luscious smile he'd dreamt about for so long. He couldn't move. He was desperate to be with her.

She stopped directly in front of him.

She didn't take her eyes off him, "Hi, Owen."

He started what became a smile, "Hi, Riley."

"Is that what I get after all this time?"

"To be honest, I wasn't expecting to run into you, so I hadn't had time to think about what to say."

"You mean a year wasn't enough time to find the right words for me?"

"Well, you did surprise me showing up like this. That's for sure."

"So, you didn't notice me following you into the parking lot?"

He looked down for a second then up at her, "No. I didn't see you come in."

"I miss you, Owen."

"I miss you, too, Riley."

The two of them went silent as they looked into each other's eyes.

Then he said, "I'm shaking. How about you?"

"Shaking? Yeah. I'm very nervous."

"You are still the most beautiful woman I've ever known. Even more so now. I see you've lost some weight. Am I right?"

"What did you expect? I haven't eaten for a year, so I'm down almost three sizes. I guess being away from you for so long has had its rewards."

"You lost weight because of us?"

"Bet your ass I did. Did you think I'd stop loving you just because you said it was over?"

"No. Not really. But, we had to stop. We were hurting too many people."

"But, we hurt ourselves, too. I know that's selfish to say. But in a situation like ours, some people have to end up hurt and some people have to end up happy. There are no other outcomes."

He couldn't take his eyes off her as she continued, "My daughters hate me more than ever. Jase continues to call me a whore in front of them. The only real solution for me is a divorce. Honey, my love for you has grown stronger and deeper, if that's possible. I think about you constantly. I worry about you."

"I know. I'm going through the same thing. My love for you has never stopped. Julie knows it, too. I've spent a lot of time just randomly driving around town hoping to see you. I never thought we'd actually meet like this."

She spread her arms and looked around, "And, yet, here we are."

"God, you're beautiful. All I want to do right now is kiss you."

"Oh, really? Just like that? In front of the bottle-return? How romantic. No, not here and not yet. Here's the deal. I'll let you kiss me, but you have to call me first."

"That's it? All I have to do is call you?"

"Jesus, Owen! You haven't called me even once. So, that's the deal. If you really want to kiss me then you have to call me at the salon tomorrow at noon."

She put her hand on his, squeezed it, and turned to leave.

Before she could walk away, he stopped her, "You know what's going to happen if I call you?"

"I do. And, we'll both be happy, again."

The next day at noon, Owen called the salon.

Sammy answered, "Good afternoon. Looking Glass Salon. How can I help you?"

"Hi. Is Riley available?"

"Yes, I'll get her for you. Hold on."

She raised the phone up so Riley could see she had a call, "It's for you, Riley."

She picked up the phone at her desk, "Hello. This is Riley Reed."

Owen started to shake, "Hi. It's me."

She'd been waiting all morning long, desperate for his call, "I was afraid you'd chicken out on me. Hold on a second while I move into the breakroom."

She excused herself from her client and walked into the breakroom.

With better privacy, she restarted the conversation, "So, tell me what's going on?"

"I miss you, Riley. It's been so long. And, I..."

She interrupted him, "I've been so unhappy, Owen. I wanted you to call me so much. Why haven't you called before now?"

"It's been very difficult. I couldn't call you. You have to understand that."

She raised her voice, "But, I needed to hear your voice. I've been going crazy without you."

"I've been going crazy, too. Months ago, I realized that I love you more than I ever knew was possible."

"You mean you didn't really love me before that?"

He knew what he'd said was wrong, "That's not what I meant. Of course, I loved you. I'm still madly in love with you."

"Then, if you really love me, why did you end it?"

"Riley, remember that I told you I was in your way. I was causing you and your family all that pain. It had to end for your own happiness and for theirs."

"Well, that didn't work out at all. My whole family is disgusted with me! Jase controls me even more, and I can't go anywhere without his permission. My love for you has not gone away and being apart has made me miserable."

"I'm sorry, Riley. I've been miserable, too. I'm having a very difficult time getting on with my life without you in it."

They both went silent for just a moment.

"How are your daughters? Is Lauren doing all right?"

"She's not doing well at all and probably will not do very well for the rest of her life. To add to that, she and her sister hate me more than ever. Jase has seen to that. He's such a wretched man. I despise him."

Owen realized that instead of getting out of her way, he should have gone in the other direction. Ending their affair did not stop the hurt for Riley, her family, or himself.

"I've really screwed this up. Haven't I?"

"Okay. That's one way to put it. I've screwed it up, too."

His eyebrows popped, "Oh? What did you do?"

"Remember I once asked Jase if we could have an open relationship?"

"Yeah. That was pretty dumb, wasn't it? As I recall, I told you I wouldn't like sharing you with him, either."

"Well, he still hasn't gotten over that one. He has no faith in me, whatsoever. He's absolutely certain that I'm going to have another affair, either back with you or with someone else. And, he's got everyone in his family, and my daughters, watching me. I should've gotten a divorce a long time ago."

"Me, too."

She asked, "So, where do we go from here?"

"I think we should talk some more. But, not over the phone. I need to see you."

She pressed him, "Are you sure that's what you want?"

He nodded, "Yes, I'm certain of it. I know it's crazy, but I have to see you. I have to touch you. I have to hold you, no matter what happens next."

Riley thought to herself, *"This is nuts. What am I gonna' do? If we start over, it'll just make me more miserable if he leaves me again. I can't take the pain any longer. If we get back together, I know what's going to happen. And, it will be wonderful!"*

She let go, "Okay, let's do it. How about noon the day after tomorrow. Shall we make it at our old spot up in Biddeford? I'll bring lunch. But, there's one condition."

"Can I guess? No hank panky?"

"You got it, mister. I'm a good girl. And, remember I'm still a virgin, so let's keep it that way."

Riley hung up the phone and couldn't stop crying.

42

The Restart

Two days later, Riley was parked behind Planet Fitness.

She thought, *"Hurry, Owen! I can't bear another minute without you."*

Just then, Owen pulled up next to her, smiled, and got out. He got in her passenger seat and closed the door.

He barely settled in before she wrapped her arms around him. She hugged him with all her strength, squeezing him until he could hardly breath.

"Oh, God. I love you so much!"

He wrapped his arms around her, "I love you, too, Riley. And, I'm not going to let go of you this time."

They kissed for the first time in over a year. It was a sensuous, intimate kiss. It was a lingering kiss, full of intense passion. Their lips were moving to a synchronized rhythm. And, their bodies flowed together. It was a kiss they'd never forget for the rest of their lives.

He stopped to look into her face, "Help me out here. Did you, or did you not, say no hanky-panky?"

"That would be a 'no' to hanky-panky."

"No? I distinctly heard you say 'yes' to hanky-panky when we were on the phone the other day. I woke up this morning with a large bulge in my pajama bottoms just dreaming about today."

She turned her face into a question mark, "You wear pajamas to bed? Really? I thought you slept naked. You're certainly not the man I knew."

"I'm still me. Believe me. So, is there going to be hanky-panky or not?"

"No, mister. Not today. We're just here to talk. Remember?"

Deflated, yet smiling, he sat back in the seat then bent forward to Riley, "What's this world coming to anyway? How about if we just touch body parts for a minute or two? I'll even let you go first."

"Hey! Snap out of it. We need to get serious, now."

He tilted his head down and feigned sadness.

She continued, "It's for certain that we still love each other and can't let go. We were hurting our families, and we tried hard to end it. But, it didn't fix the problems. So, what do we do now?"

"There's no question. I just know we need to get back together. And, we can keep it a secret better than we did before. We still have our TracFones. I get my haircut at Tony's now. We've got plenty of love codes and a great meeting spot. Don't forget, we have a floating hotel room. As long as we're extra careful, we can pull it off. Nobody will get hurt."

"But, Jase and his entire family are watching me every minute. I can't go anywhere without one of them reporting in. They're probably watching us right now, for God sake."

Owen looked around and saw nothing unusual, "Nope, we're clear. The trick will be to keep from using the same schedule or location. We'll need to find better places to meet. We'll need to be careful when going and coming on *Airship*. And, if someone challenges us, deny everything. Never admit to what we're doing. Just brush it off."

"But, you know I'm a horrible liar. This is going to be difficult."

Before leaving, they ate the lunch Riley had brought with her then hugged and kissed each other goodbye.

They drove off in opposite directions, each with a huge smile.

They failed to see the green pickup truck parked across the road from the Shopping Center.

A week later, Owen found a parking lot used by Aaron Enterprises, the largest company in Wells. It was far from the beach and tourist areas and surrounded by dense forest. There were lots of cars in the lot, but there was an empty area in one corner. There were no security cameras, and the lot could only be entered or exited from a quarter-mile, narrow road leading from the highway. It was perfect.

They planned ahead for the days and times that they'd be together with a mix of routes and a varied schedule. No one would ever be able to find them.

Their first visit was an exciting and intimate one. Their spot was empty so they parked their cars next to each other at the edge of the forest directly in front of them.

Riley climbed into the back seat. He got out and joined her.

Owen reached out to hold her hand. They didn't talk. They leaned toward each other. They touched then kissed. It was a gentle kiss. It was soft and tender, and a bit playful at first. They smiled. She giggled. They became more focused. He nibbled at her neck. She slid her tongue across his ear. He ran his fingers past her lips. They kissed again. It became more intense.

The only thing the two of them were thinking about was the love they shared so long ago. It was time to catch up to where they'd been.

She stopped and told him, "I love you, Owen Flynn. I've been desperate for you for way too long. I need you. I want to become a part of you. The deep and exciting part of who you are."

"I love you, too. I've missed you so very much. You're all I've thought about. I won't let you go again. You are my life, now."

From their secluded hideaway, they were completely free. They were fully alone and free to declare their love for each other. They didn't need to state it in words. It was in their eyes, in their lips, and in their hearts.

It didn't take long for them to be completely immersed in each other. They moved together as one. It was a pulsating, rhythmic flow, yet full of tenderness. Their motion was easy and slow, at times. Then, it became strong and passionate.

Their love-making ended after an hour. They held tight to each other, pledging never to let go.

She began to cry softly, "What are we going to do now, Owen? Honey?"

He responded, "I don't know. We'll have to come up with something. Whatever it is, we'll be together now. I promise you that."

They made time to spend with each other over the next four months. At times, it was in the Aaron parking lot, behind Planet Fitness, or onboard *Airship*. During the coming spring, the expected tourist crowds helped camouflage their movements.

The times they spent together involved much more than just love-making. They laughed a lot. They teased each other. They told stories about themselves. They learned more about each other every day, and what they learned was fun and exciting. And, they talked about their future.

"I wish we were living together," she told him.

"You mean like we were married or something?"

"Married? I'm not sure about that just yet. After all, when I'm only sixty, you'll be eighty-five. Yuck! I never imagined I'd ever make love to an eighty-five-year-old man."

"I never thought I'd make love to a sixty-year-old woman, either."

They laughed together then got serious, "I do plan on making love with you when I'm eighty-five. Maybe even after I turn a hundred."

"But, what if your penis becomes all wrinkled and stuff?"

"Not a problem. I expect they'll have some new pill for us senile old men to take by then."

"But, I'll probably have to wake you up first."

Week after week, they were confident that their renewed affair was a secret. No one at the salon knew, except Crystal. No phone calls were made, except on their TracFones. They varied their meeting times and places. She was vigilant to keep Jase informed of where she went and was quick to answer her cell phone whenever he called.

Owen managed his wife's thoughts, as well. He showered her with affection, but not love. He kept her informed of his whereabouts and was quick to respond to her calls, too. He had an answer for any challenge from Julie, just in case.

The deception was working. But, only for a while.

43

The Secret

Owen arrived at work early.

After a few minutes, his office phone rang. Riley's number popped up on the display.

He picked up the phone and greeted her right away, "Hey. How are you, Honey?"

"I'm okay. At least I think so for now. I'm a little anxious about something we haven't talked about."

"Uh oh, what's that? You all right?"

"Yeah, I'm all right. But, I really don't want to talk about it over the phone. Can I see you up in Biddeford?"

"Of course. But, not today. How about Friday?"

"That's a good day for me, too. Let's get there at noon. Okay?"

"That's noon on Friday up in Biddeford. Okay. And, Riley, whatever it is that's wrong, trust that we can fix it. Except death, so I hope you didn't kill anybody."

"I haven't killed anybody yet, but I should have."

On Friday, they met again. It was raining.

He opened her door, "Hi, Honey. Sorry that it's a bit dreary today. Let's get in the backseat."

They jumped in the back and closed the doors. They moved close together and clung to each other. They didn't let go. They fully enjoyed the depth of the love they felt together.

He stopped and pulled back, "So, tell me. What's wrong?"

"Nothing's really wrong. I just need to tell you something about me that I think you should know. It's about my past."

"I thought I knew everything about you. What have I missed?"

"This is a bit serious. It won't affect us, but I want to be open with you all the way. So, here goes."

She took a deep breath, "When I was seven, my neighbor sexually molested me. He was twenty-two."

Shocked, Owen couldn't help but respond, "Jesus, Riley! For real?"

"Unfortunately, it is for real. His name was Danny McGregor. It went on for over six years. Christ, I had my first orgasm when I was ten."

Owen was startled at the news, "Riley, you aren't kidding, are you? That had to be..."

She interrupted him, "That's not all. After a couple of years, my step-father found out what was going on, so he molested me, too."

"Oh, my God! What did your mother do when she found out?"

"Well, I tried to tell her a few times, but she never believed me. She wouldn't listen to me at all."

"That's not possible! How does she explain herself? What was she doing when this was happening to you?"

"It was always at my neighbor's house, so she never saw anything. They did it to me two or three times a week."

"Goddamn them! Wait a minute. You were always at your neighbor's house with your step-father, and your mother didn't figure out that something bad might be going on over there? Why didn't she ask you, or your neighbor, or her husband why the Hell you were over there so much?"

"I don't know. She was so busy at the prison. She was a nurse up there. She just didn't have time for me."

"So, your mother was a nurse at the prison when her husband should have been an inmate there?"

Riley, choked back a bit, "Yeah, I know."

"So, what happened? What ended it?"

"Well, my step-father tried to molest my other sister, Annie, too. When she told Mom about it, Mom finally believed me and called the police. They were both found guilty. My neighbor went to prison and my step-father just took off and disappeared somewhere in Florida. We never saw them again."

Owen needed more answers to his questions, "Is your neighbor still in prison?"

"He has to be. I wasn't his only victim. He went after other girls in town, too. His son, Fred, contacted me a few years ago and told me that his father tried to commit suicide. It scares me every time I think about him. But, I'm safe while he rots in jail."

"Are you okay with all this? It's got to have hurt you deeply."

"Don't worry. I'm okay. I know this sounds crazy, but I got over it a long time ago. I have to tell you, though, that I haven't forgiven my mother. Why the fuck didn't she believe me when I told her the first time. It took Annie being attacked before she did anything about it."

"I hate to say this, but your mother had to have known all along that something was happening next door. She should have gone to prison with your neighbor."

"Yup. I figured that out a long time ago. Today, she won't talk about it at all. It's as if it never happened."

"That's because she knows she's guilty. Is there anything I can do for you... other than strangling your mother?"

"No, it's too late for that. Just put your arms around me and hold me tight as often as you can."

"That'll be easy. I'll take good care of you, Riley Reed."

"You know something?"

"What?"

"I believe you really will take good care of me."

Riley was suddenly concerned, "Did I frighten you just now?"

"Of course not. I'm glad that you thought enough of me to tell me what happened to you."

"I told you I'm okay. Please don't worry about me. Jase thinks it was all my fault."

Owen shook his head in disbelief, "How can he possibly think that you had anything to do with that? You were only seven years old, for God sake."

"It's his mother. She's freakin' nuts. She told Jase not to marry me because I, quote, 'have a problem.' He's used it against me for years."

"Have your daughters ever heard him say that to you?"

"Of course. It's one of his ways he uses to control me. Basically, if I don't say or act the way he wants, he reminds me of 'my problem' in front of the girls."

Owen was pissed at Jase, "You know why he's doing it? It's his way of being superior to you. If he can make them see you as a flawed mother then he believes they'll love him more than they love you."

"I've felt that ever since my girls were in high school. He does it with my family, too. Why does he want to be superior to me?"

"Because he's an asshole! Better put, he's not a smart man at all. He doesn't want people to think you're better or smarter than he is."

She started to cry, put her head in her hands, and bent forward, "I don't know what to do. My daughters hate me so much, and they won't listen to me at all."

He put his arms around her and pulled her close, "I don't know either. What I do know is that someday Jase is going to make a mistake, and your girls will see him for who he really is. They'll come back to you then. You just need to be patient."

They spent the next half hour just wrapped around each other. They didn't talk. Their hearts were beating fast and strong.

They realized that their relationship was consuming them, yet they also feared what lay ahead.

44

The Discovery

A few days later, Julie was picking up the bedroom.

Owen's clothes from the day before were laying in a pile on the chest at the foot of their bed. She grabbed his underwear and shirt then placed them in the hamper. When she picked up his suit pants, she searched his pockets. She took out a used handkerchief and added it to the pile. She found a couple of notes relating to his work and placed them on his dresser.

When she went to hang his suit pants, she took hold of the cuffs and turned the pants upside down. Something fell out of a back pocket. The sound of hard plastic hitting the floor startled her.

She looked down and found a TracFone at her feet, "W*hat the Hell is that?"*

She picked it up and turned it around in her hands, *"It's a cell phone. It's not his regular cell phone. This is different."*

A hundred thoughts ran through her head, *"This must be his work phone. But, wait a minute. He uses a different cell phone for work."*

She was curious to find out what was going on. She turned it on to browse the history of calls he'd made. There was only one number that'd been called or received over many different dates.

She sensed a problem, *"I don't ever remember him using this phone. And, why has he called only one number?"*

She decided that the only way to find out who he'd been calling was to call the number. So, she turned the phone on and pressed the button for a callback.

It rang three times before Riley answered it, "Hi, Honey. What's goin' on?"

Julie pressed the 'off' button immediately then lost her grip on the phone. It fell to the floor.

"My God! That bitch! They're at it again."

Later that day, Owen arrived home from work. Julie had been pacing around the kitchen table.

Zeke greeted him at the door. When he looked up after petting his canine buddy, he found Julie staring at him. She was speechless.

"Hi. Is everything all right? You look a little troubled."

She continued to stare at her husband. She didn't say a word.

He straightened up from Zeke and walked to the other side of the table. He sat down facing her.

He put his hands together on the table and tried to talk with her once again, "What's wrong?"

Her eyes started to tear up, "What are you up to?"

"I don't know what you mean."

"You're at it again, aren't you?"

He sensed what was coming, but didn't let on, "I'm not sure what you're talking about. What have I done?"

She opened her hand to show him the TracFone that she'd found in his pocket.

When he saw it, a shock ran through his body, *"Shit!"*

Julie demanded, "You want to explain this?"

He attempted to recover, "It's easy to explain. It's my new cell phone for work. United changed the vendor for their phones. That's all."

With her emotions in check, she calmly but clearly told him the truth, "I don't think so, Owen. I checked the call history, and there's only one number that's been called at all from this phone. It was easy to find out who you've been calling. When I called the number, she answered thinking it was her 'Honey.' That would be you."

Julie threw the phone at him. It fell to the floor. He picked it up and looked at it.

He thought for a few seconds then faced the reality of the situation. He had no defense. No explanation. No more lies to tell.

He hung his head and wiped the sweat accumulating on his forehead, "I'm sorry, Julie. This has been very..."

"That's enough. There's no way to explain what's going on. It's simple. You love her. You don't love me."

"It's not about you."

"Bullshit. Of course, it's about me. You've chosen her over me. So, it's over for us. I'm getting a divorce. You need to leave now. Right now! Get out!"

"Julie, sweetheart. You've got this all wrong."

"I said, get out. I never want to see your face again!"

She cried uncontrollably.

Owen went to the bedroom to retrieve a suitcase and some clothes. When he was finished, he put the phone in his pocket and went back downstairs to the kitchen.

Before he could get out the door, she screamed, "And, take this fucking dog with you."

Reluctantly, Owen connected Zeke's harness and leash then opened the door with his dog in tow. They got into his car and drove to the yacht club. Depressed by the situation, he and Zeke climbed aboard *Airship*.

He put his clothes and things in the aft berth then went into the forward berth. Zeke followed as they both climbed onto the bed.

"Fuck. This is a disaster!

Julie was outraged. She couldn't believe that Owen would give up his home and his life for that retched woman. The bitch! What spell did she have over him? Was it her age? It had to be. She was so much younger. But, other than that, Julie could find no clear explanation for Owen's behavior.

She continued to ponder what'd just happened to her, *"What a miserable day. I've had it with him. And, with her!"*

And, what about Riley's husband? Did he know that his wife's affair was back on?

He needed to know.

She looked up Jason Reed's home number on the Internet then called him.

"Hello."

"Is this Jason Reed?"

"Yes, this is Jason. Who's this?"

"This is Julie Flynn. I'm Owen Flynn's wife. I assume you know him?"

He hesitated for a moment, "Yes. I know who he is. What's this all about?"

"I just want you to know that I just threw my husband out of our house. He's been spending time with your wife."

"Well, they were seeing each other. But, that stopped a long time ago."

"I know. But, they've started back up again. I don't know all the details, but they must be back spending time together now. They've got secret cell phones that I found. I called the number on my husband's phone and your wife answered thinking it was him. They've been cheating on us!"

Jase was furious, "I'll go talk to her right now. I'll find out what the fuck they're doing. Damn it!"

They hung up without another word.

As soon as the call from Julie was over, Jase ran to the basement where Riley was working out on the treadmill.

Outraged, he demanded, "You've been seeing that asshole Flynn again. Haven't you?"

"Of course not. Why would you even ask?"

"So, let me get this straight. You don't see him? You don't talk to him? You don't connect with him in any way at all?"

She stopped the treadmill and rested her hands on the handles, "Why are you getting all worked up over something that ended a long time ago? I told you it was over. I told you I made a mistake. I apologized for it and promised I'd never do it again."

"Do you happen to have some special phone that I don't know about?"

"Shit! How does he know about our phones?"

She lied to him again, "Special phones? I have no idea what you're talking about."

"I just got a call from Julie Flynn. Owen's wife? She told me that she found some secret phone in Owen's pocket. She threw him out of the house because he admitted that your affair with him was back on."

"Well, that's just crazy. We aren't..."

He grabbed her by the throat once more, pulled her off the treadmill, and slammed her against the clothes washer. She struggled to get free, but he was too strong. He squeezed her windpipe. She choked for air. She kicked him swift and hard in the groin. He doubled over in pain. He let go of her neck.

She used the chance to get away from her husband and ran for the cellar stairs. But, he tackled her on the fourth step. She slammed down hard as he pulled her down to him. He flipped her over.

"You goddamn bitch. I told you what would happen if you didn't stop this shit. I'm going to kill him then I'm coming back for you."

Kelly, heard her Dad yelling at her mother again. She ran to the kitchen and stood in the open cellar doorway. She looked down to see her Dad holding her Mom against the stairs and screaming.

"Daddy? You've got to stop doing this to Mom!"

He kept his hands on Riley as he looked up at his older daughter, "Your fucking mother is at it again. I told you and your sister that she was a whore. Nothing has changed. I'll deal with this. Just go back to your room!"

Before Kelly left the kitchen, she yelled down to her mother, "Ma, why are you trying to hurt us, again? We're through with you. You can just go to Hell. I don't want you to be our mother anymore!"

Kelly spun around and ran back upstairs, crying.

Jase let go of Riley and raced up the stairs after his daughter.

Riley knew she had to get out of the house and tell Owen what had happened. She needed to warn him.

She grabbed her coat, purse, and car keys then ran out the kitchen door.

She drove to the only place she thought she might find Owen, the yacht club.

When she entered the parking lot, she was relieved to see his car. She parked and ran down the ramp to *Airship*. The cockpit hatch door was open and light was shining up through it.

She boarded and called down to him, "Owen? It's me."

Zeke barked at her from the galley below. Owen climbed the ladder to find her crying, now sitting on the edge of the cockpit. He sat next to her and put his arms around her.

"What's happened? Why are you crying?"

"Jase tried to choke me again, and it was really bad. Oh, Honey, what's worse is that my daughters are fed up with me, now. They know that I've been lying to them about us. Kelly just told me that they didn't want me as their mother anymore."

He pulled her closer, "I am so sorry about your kids. You don't deserve any of this. Someday they'll discover that you've been a good mother to them. Until that happens, it's going to be very hard on you. And, me, too. As for Jase, that bastard. Are you okay? What made him so mad this time?"

"It was our phones. Apparently, your wife found your phone. Then, according to Jase, she called him with it…"

"Goddamn it! Why the Hell did she do that?"

"My guess is she was really pissed off. She's such a bitch. She wanted to hurt us, and I'd say she did a good job of it."

"She sure did. And, she threw me out of the house, too. Zeke and I are down here to stay until we find a place on land."

"I can't go back home. Jase said he's going to kill us. First you then me. I know he's said this before, but this time he's really gone crazy. But, if we stay on *Airship* he'll find us for sure. We've got to get out of here."

"No, he won't. I'm going to move *Airship* down the coast a way to a marina in Wells. It's at the end of Harbor Road. How about if you drive down and meet me there later?"

"You sure you want to do this?"

"I've never been so sure of anything in my life. We need to stay together, and our best option right now is *Airship* in Wells. Nobody'll find us there. You know where Harbor Road is?"

"Yeah. I do."

"Okay. It won't take me long to motor down there. Can you stop at a grocery store to get some food for us? And, make sure you get plenty of wine. I think we're going to need it."

"Agreed. It's time to get drunk!"

45

The Terror

When *Airship* put in at the marina in Wells, Riley was there waiting.

She'd parked her car in the only open spot about fifty-feet from the dock. The trunk was full of groceries.

Owen finished tying up *Airship* then walked to her car. When she got out, they held onto each other and were silent for nearly five minutes.

He was first to speak, "I'm so sorry, Honey. I guess I blew it again."

"What do you mean?"

"The TracFone. I left it in my pants pocket by mistake."

She smiled at him, "Is there a problem here?"

He looked hard at her face then questioned her, "Well, I thought so. What're you saying?"

"Let's see. You and I love each other more deeply than anyone else in the world. Both of us suffered for the time we weren't together. I hate my husband. You hate your wife. We're both free now. No more lies. No more hiding. No more TracFones. This is exactly where we need to be. Just the two of us. Together."

Owen thought for an instant, smiled at Riley, and added, "It's not just the two of us. We have Zeke, too."

They took the groceries out of her car, went back aboard *Airship*, and went below.

The Dachshund was sitting on the salon bench waiting for them. Riley sat next to him. She put her arm across Zeke's back and bent down to hug him. He whined a bit then licked her face.

Riley smiled and looked up at Owen, "I've wanted to meet him for so long. We'll have to go back to the grocery store to get dog food and treats for him."

"He's going to love you for that."

After shopping for Zeke's food, they returned to the marina.

Back onboard the boat again, Riley opened the grocery bags and found places to put all the food that she'd bought. Zeke was handed a snack then waddled through the passageway to the forward berth and jumped up on the bed.

Riley sat on the port-side bench and quietly watched Owen move about the cabin. He took a cork screw out of a compartment in the galley wall and opened one of the bottles of wine. He poured two glasses then sat back again next to her on the bench.

She was deep in thought.

Owen was anxious, "You okay?"

"Yeah. I'm okay. Don't worry. I'm just thinking about what just happened and wondering what's going to happen next. It's scary."

Her regular cell phone started to ring. She got up and retrieved it from her purse. She looked at the Caller ID. It was Jase. She turned her phone off to stop the call.

"That was Jase. He obviously wants to know where I am. I don't want to talk to him."

"Maybe you should talk to him. Just don't tell him where you are."

She was shaking. Owen got up and put his arms around her. He held her tight.

"I'm scared. He's so mad. I really don't know what he'll do."

Owen pulled her back and looked past the tears in her eyes, "He's not going to kill us. He just wants to scare us, that's all. We have to be tough and ignore what he says."

Jase called again.

Owen suggested, "Take a deep breath. And, don't get angry at him."

She looked at her phone before she answered it, "Hello, Jase."

Jase could tell in her voice that she was scared, "Hi, Riley. I'm sorry that I got so upset. I know I hurt you. Are you okay?"

"I have a few bruises. Nothing's broken. But, it hurts anyway."

"Where are you? When will you be back?"

"I'm not going back. For God sake, you hurt me and tried to kill me. Again! That was it for me. I can't trust you anymore."

"That's crazy, Riley. You know me. I just got a little emotional that's all. I wouldn't hurt you, and you know that."

"Jase, you already have hurt me. I told you I can't trust you at all."

He turned livid and screamed, "You bitch! You come back home right now! I know where to find you. It'll be a lot worse for you if I have to go get you. Come home now."

"No. Jase. It's all over. I'm never going back to you. I want a divorce."

She hung up on him then sat next to Owen on the bench and cried.

"He threatened me again just now. He wants to hurt me. I can't go back."

"What about your daughters?"

"I want them to be with me. But, Jase has poisoned their minds so much, I'm not so sure they want to be with me at all."

"There's plenty of room on *Airship* for them. They might like living with us."

She shook her head, "I don't think so, Honey. They hate you even more than they hate me. Jase's got them believing that you stole me away from them."

"I stole you away? No, how about, he pushed you away!"

"Look. I just want my girls to be able to visit me at any time. I'm going to get an apartment first, that'll give me time to look for a house."

He finished the last sip of his wine then added, "I understand. We'll make this work for us for as long as we can. It may take a while before we're out of the woods, but we'll be all right. You'll see."

She smiled, cuddled close, and kissed him, "I need you in my life. I can't do this without you. I need your strength, your love, your passion, your touch. I need you there with me when the world unravels. And, if you think the difference in our age matters at all, know this. I plan to be with you forever. I don't care what our ages are because your love is the youngest and richest love I could ever have. I know that there's no one else in this world that I would rather be with for the rest of my life. I want to marry you when this is all over."

Owen couldn't speak. He held her hands and bowed his head slightly to kiss them.

After a few minutes, she added, "What do you say we go to bed? And, let's put Zeke in the back of the boat."

"You mean aft?"

"Shut up and kiss me. Then pour me some more wine."

46

The Apartment

The next morning, Riley told Owen she was going to look for an apartment.

He asked, "Can you drop me off at my car first? It's back at the yacht club in Kennebunkport. I'll need it so I can get around."

"Oh, yeah. I almost forgot. Of course, I will. But, don't you want to go apartment hunting with me? I expect you'll be spending a lot of time there, so you're going to have a say in which one I get."

"Thanks. I'd like to go with you. Let's go get my car first. Then, we'll go apartment hunting. Okay?"

She nodded agreement and headed for her car with Owen close behind. He sped up to her, so they could hold hands.

They drove out of the marina and north to Kennebunkport.

She started to get nervous as they got closer to town. "Hey. What if Jase is waiting for us in the parking lot? I'm pretty sure he found out long ago where you kept your boat."

"Let's be careful. There's another entrance to the yacht club lot that few people know about. I'll use that one, and we can see if he's there before we go in."

He was nervous, too. It had become clear to him that Jase was actually crazy. He wanted to kill Owen. So, did Julie. So, did her daughters. Riley's mother-in-law, too. Her sister. It was the whole damn family! A whole lot of people could be waiting for them. They'd have to stay calm and look before they approached his car.

When they got to the yacht club, he pointed out the private entrance. They turned off Ocean Avenue and slowly moved along the road that went around the club house. There were shrubs that provided a good place to stop and hide before they checked out the parking lot.

It was all clear.

Owen got out of Riley's car and walked quickly toward his. She watched to see when he got in, ready to leave.

But, while she was watching him, he suddenly stopped, and crouched down.

She thought he must have seen someone near his car, *"Fuck! What's going on?"*

He looked around. There was no one else in the lot that he could see. But, there was a problem. A big problem. He waved at Riley to come join him. She got out and quickly caught up to him.

"What's the matter?"

He pointed to his car in front of them. Its windows were smashed. All of them. Even the windshield.

They looked at each other with fear in their eyes.

She quietly told him, "Let's get the Hell out of here, right now."

She grabbed his hand then pulled him back toward her car. They ran. When they got to the car, they jumped in either side.

She backed out and stopped at Ocean Avenue. When the road cleared, they headed south out of town.

It was more than two miles before either of them said a word.

Owen was first to talk, "So, you wanna get some breakfast?"

"Holy shit, Honey. I told you Jase's going to try to kill us. I just know it."

"Let's get some breakfast first then we can talk."

"I told you he was nuts. My God, what're we going to do now?"

"I said, we're going to go have breakfast."

"Breakfast? I'm going to throw up if I have breakfast. Didn't you see your car? He smashed all the windows."

"Why do you think it's Jase. It could be anyone in your family. Mine, too."

Speeding south, Owen told her, "I'm going to have Andy Warren pick up my car and put in new windows. It'll take a few days to fix it and get it back to me. Problem solved."

"Problem solved? Yeah, your car will be fixed. What about everything else?"

"Look. We don't know who did this, right? Maybe it was Jase. Maybe not. What's important right now is that we have to be really careful. I don't trust anyone at all anymore. Except you."

They pulled into The Donut Hole for breakfast. They parked, went inside, and sat side-by-side in the only booth available.

The waitress greeted them, "Hi, I'm Katy. Want some coffee while you're looking over the menu?"

Riley answered for them, "Yes, please, Katy. That would be fine. We'll need some cream and sugar, too."

Katy handed a menu to them then explained, "The specials are on the wall next to the kitchen. The French Toast is a big favorite."

They tried to look at the menu choices, but their brains were not processing all that was happening. In between buttermilk pancakes and waffles, Riley imagined Jase coming at her with a knife. It was truly a living nightmare.

She was frantic beyond belief and thought to herself, *"Who is doing this? What's next? When? Where? Is Jase really out to kill us? Are they going to run us off the road and into a tree? For Christ sake, these days most marriages get into trouble, just like ours. Why can't they all just let this go?"*

Katy arrived with their coffees, "So, what can I get for you this morning?"

With her brain off elsewhere, Riley tried to order, "Oh, I don't know. How about an egg omelette?"

Both Owen and Katy had a good laugh.

Katy was still giggling when she told Riley, "Yes. Every one of our omelettes is an egg omelette. What would you like us to put in it?"

Riley shook her head and smiled, "Sorry about that. I'll have a three-cheese Omelette and a jelly donut for dessert, please."

Still grinning, Owen ordered the French Toast and added a side of scrambled eggs.

Katy picked up the menus and, before returning to the kitchen, said, "Thanks, you two. That was fun."

After they finished their breakfast, they drove into Wells. Along the way, Owen called Warren's Garage. He asked Andy to use his tow truck again to go pick up his car at the yacht club. This time to replace all its windows.

Andy was surprised, "Did you say replace the glass in all the windows? What kind of accident were you in?"

"It wasn't an accident. Just more teenagers messing around with me, again."

"Want me to call the police for ya'?"

He lied to Andy, "No. But, thanks anyway. I already took care of it."

After Andy told him it would take three days to put in new windows, they hung up.

Riley looked at Owen, "You wanna look at apartments with me. Right?"

"Absolutely. Where do we start?"

She told him she had a manicure client who was a real estate agent in Wells.

They drove to her office and went inside. Betty Thompson looked up and saw Riley walk in with a man who appeared to be her father.

She jumped up from behind her desk and threw her hands into the air, "Hey, Riley. What're you doing here? You and Jase finally looking to move?"

Riley walked over and hugged Betty, "Is there an office where we can talk?"

Betty changed her excitement to a soft smile, "Yup. Just follow me."

Along the way, Betty gave a quick hello to Owen.

Riley realized her mistake and introduced her to him, "I'm sorry, Betty. This is Owen Flynn. He and I are together."

Betty choked silently, hiding her reaction to what she had just been told.

"Hello, Mr. Flynn. I'm happy to meet you."

Betty showed them into a small office with a table surrounded by four chairs.

As she closed the door, she said, "There. We'll have all the privacy we need. Why don't you tell me why you're here?"

"Okay. Here we go. We need an apartment somewhere around Wells. Let's start with privacy and security. I don't want anyone breaking in on us. And, I need a big bedroom with a good-sized bathroom. The living room should be comfortable. Internet with Wi-Fi, cable TV, central air, laundry, and a pool."

Betty had been taking notes, "I guess you've been thinking about this for a while. Huh?"

"Not really."

The three of them looked over several pages of photos of apartments in and around Wells. Betty covered the features and amenities of each and showed them the monthly rent. They picked four of them that appeared to meet Riley's needs.

After thirty minutes of questions and answers, they broke the list down to just two apartments. Betty invited them to go with her to check them out.

Riley asked Owen what he thought about what they'd seen so far. He told her what he liked and didn't like about each. He was very frank and clear with his advice.

In the end, they agreed on the second apartment. It had one large bedroom and a slightly smaller one. There was a modest-sized bathroom and one with the second bedroom. It had a big kitchen with up-to-date appliances and a very large living room. There were a lot of windows providing ample light. There was a centrally-monitored, security system, central air, Wi-Fi, and cable TV.

The setting was perfect. It was an old garment factory with brick walls that'd been converted to modern apartments. The lobby was a massive, three-story structure. Outside there was an Olympic-sized pool and facilities for outdoor barbecuing. The trees, grass, flower gardens, and plantings were immaculate. There was also a fitness center with an indoor exercising pool in the manager's office building. And, it was private and secure. Perfect for two lovers starting out together, trying to stay alive.

After more discussion and a few more questions, Riley decided to take the apartment and signed the lease agreement. She handed Betty a signed check for the first two months and a security deposit. The apartment manager gave her the keys. She also gave her a list of amenities.

Finally, the manager gave her a long list of rules for the apartment with warnings about marijuana, illegal drugs, harassment, fist fights, open liquor bottles, setting fires in the workout room, stealing tenants' underwear, peeing in the sink, and a special note about a game called 'Limp Frog.' Apparently, there was a considerable number of young-adult tenants in the complex.

Riley didn't have time to read the rest of the rules and gave them to Owen.

Over the next several weeks, they went shopping for furniture. Owen helped with her selections. He found her tastes to be both exceptional and expensive. He cautioned her to keep from becoming 'House Poor,' but his words were not heard at all. She examined window dressings for hours. He found places to sit while she conducted her searches. When she'd found something she liked, she called Owen over for his opinion. They found it both odd and interesting that the two of them liked exactly the same things in a home.

Another week went by, she was ready to move in to her new apartment. Owen had just finished the last touches in her bedroom and met her in the middle of her new living room.

She put her hands on his shoulders and started to cry, "I know you wanted me to stay on *Airship* with you and Zeke, but I have to do this. I know you'll understand when I explain that I need more. I need space. I need a walk-in closet, a bathroom with a shower and a tub, a big kitchen to do all my cooking, and a living room that's more than ten feet wide. And, I want my daughters to join me here someday"

She took a deep breath, wrapped her arms around him, and continued, "Honey, I love you more than I ever knew was possible. We're not saying goodbye. Not at all. In fact, I want you here with me always. In my bed. In my arms. In my body. And, I'll be onboard *Airship* every time you set sail. I know there'll be overnights from time to time, and I'm happy to stay with you on *Airship*. I don't even get seasick, for Christ sake."

She took one of the two apartment keys the manager had given her and handed it to him, "There. Take my key and keep it with you always. I want you to come and go as if this was your apartment, too. Move your clothes into my closet. Fill the fridge with food you like. Put bottles of rum in my liquor cabinet. Use the shower. Use my towels. Make a mess... then clean it up. Being an Army veteran, you should know how to do stuff around here. So, wash our dishes. Do our laundry. Sew, but I'm not sure what that word means. Iron our clothes. Make our bed. Clean our bathroom. Hang our Christmas lights. Fix everything. And, when you're all done..."

She grabbed his hand and yanked him into the bedroom. She pushed him onto their bed and jumped on top of him,

"...help me make a mess of our bed."

47

The Divorces

It took only three weeks for Julie's divorce from Owen to run its course.

Altogether, it was relatively easy. The two of them and their lawyers went through all the joint property, bank accounts, financial assets, and belongings then came to a quick agreement. She wanted him out of her life. He wanted her out of his.

His biggest complaint was giving up the house. After all, it was a Flynn family heirloom worth over five million dollars. Monthly alimony to Julie was reasonable and ended in five years.

When Owen returned to *Airship* after the final hearing, Riley and Zeke were waiting for him at the dock.

"Hey, there. How'd it go?"

He petted Zeke while attempting a smile, "As expected, I guess. We didn't have to get into a fight about anything. I lost the house."

She shook her head, "I figured that was going to happen. You keep *Airship*, though. Right?"

"Yeah. I get to keep her. But, I want to find another house someday. Probably won't be an antique like the one I had, but it will be spacious and comfortable."

"I'd like to get another house, too. We should get one together."

"That sounds like a really good idea, but..."

Interrupting, she asked, "What do you mean 'but?'"

"Riley, I've told you before. You shouldn't be making life's decisions that include me. I'm twenty-five years older than you. The VA has given me a lot of medications to take. You need to find that guy I called Charlie who's more your age. Remember? He'll be healthy, strong, handsome, and wealthy. If you're off buying a house with me, he's going to pass right by you."

She took hold of both his hands, looked him square in his eyes, "Owen, I want you in my life and no one else. This guy you keep calling Charlie isn't going to be half the man I love. And, that man I love is standing in front of me right now. So, stop talking nonsense and kiss me."

With deep sadness in his eyes, he looked down at his dog, "And, Zeke here. I need to find him another home."

"Oh, Honey. Why?"

"'Because he won't be happy living on the boat. Kind of like you. He needs more space than I can give him now. He needs to chase Gulls and Sandpipers on the beach every day. He needs a fun, human family around him. It's going to hurt, but I'll find him a good place."

She rested her head on his shoulder, "I'm so sorry, Honey. I know how very much you love this little guy. He's like a son to you."

"Yes. I do love him like a son. I hope I can find someone close by who'll take him. Maybe they'll let me walk him on the beach every now and then."

"Maybe I can help. I'll see if anyone at the salon might be interested to take him. I know he'll miss you."

They hugged and kissed each other still standing on the dock. They turned with Zeke in tow and stepped aboard *Airship*. They went below and quietly sat together in the salon holding hands.

Owen asked her, "What about you? Any news from Jase?"

"Yup. He called me again this morning. He's still pissed off! It's very hard to talk with him. He's rambling on about killing us. He won't answer any question I ask. He's really gone off the deep end. He's scaring the Hell out of me."

"I think it's time for you to get a lawyer. Then, you can file for divorce. And, you should file, not Jase."

"That's what a client of mine told me, too. She gave me the name and number of a really good lawyer. I'll call him and see if I can get in to see him soon. My client told me it might take a while before I can meet with him."

"That's too bad. But, it's typical to wait a long time to get to talk with one. Let's hope it's not too long. We need you to be free of Jase as soon as you can."

The next day, Riley called a divorce lawyer named William Delany.

"Good morning. Attorney Delany's office."

"Hi, my name is Riley Reed. I'm hoping Mr. Delaney will help me with my divorce. I'd like to make an appointment with him, if possible."

"Thank you, Miss Reed. When would you like to meet with him?"

"The sooner the better."

"I have an hour appointment for tomorrow that just got cancelled. It's at 2:00. Would that work for you?"

"Yes. That's great. I think I have your location. Is it on Berwick Road in Ogunquit?"

"That's correct. Be sure to bring as much documentation as possible. You know, W-2s, tax returns for the past four years, lists of assets, liabilities, family information, etc. If we need anything more, Mr. Delaney will make out a list for you. We'll see you tomorrow at 2:00, then. Have a good day."

"You, too. Bye."

After she ended the call, she called Owen to tell him, "Hi, Honey. Good news! I got an attorney right away. I'm going to meet with him tomorrow at 2:00."

"That's amazing! Good for you."

It took two and a half months of meetings, debates, and arguments before Riley, Jase, and their lawyers reached a final settlement.

When she returned from the last session with the attorneys, she told Owen, "Fuck him! I'm so relieved to get rid of him."

"Did it go as you hoped it would?"

"Yes. I'm very surprised that he accepted so many of my terms. I gave up the house, but I made him think I really wanted it. We split everything down the middle. He has to give me half the value of the house, its contents, the property, my car, and all my jewelry."

"When's the court hearing?"

"It's next Tuesday. My lawyer wants to get me a good alimony settlement. I'm keeping my fingers crossed."

"So am I."

Tuesday morning Riley met Delany at the courthouse.

"Good morning, Riley. How are you doing?"

"I'm nervous. Very nervous. Please tell me this will go well for me today?"

He put his arm over her shoulder and walked her to the entrance, "You need to trust me on this, Riley. You know this is not my first day on the job. You're going to get everything we agreed on and maybe more."

They entered the courthouse and walked into the hearing room. Riley's case was second on the schedule. They took their seats. Jase and his lawyer took theirs.

After the first case was thrown out, Riley's hearing began.

The first five minutes involved the presentation of documents along with discussions between the lawyers and the judge.

When finished, Delany returned to his seat next to Riley and quietly told her, "Good news. Actually, very good news. The judge is accepting all we agreed on and given you a very nice alimony settlement. It's going to be a thousand a week for the next ten years."

Riley couldn't believe what she'd just heard!

She bent down to whisper to Delany, "Holy shit! What the Hell did you say to the judge?"

"I just pointed my finger at the salary Jase brings in each week compared to yours. It was pretty easy, frankly."

After the hearing, Riley went back to her apartment. Owen had been anxiously awaiting her return.

She walked through her door with a grim look on her face, "Hi, Honey."

Owen got up off the couch, "Uh oh! What happened? You look like you had the shit kicked out of you."

"Well, it's like this. The judge accepted all that we'd agreed on. Then, she awarded me a thousand dollars a week alimony for the next ten years!"

Owen jumped off the couch, picked Riley up off the floor, and screamed, "Holy shit, Riley. Are you kidding me? That's incredible!"

As he swung her around the living room floor, he asked, "That must have really pissed Jase off?"

"No kidding. He got so upset with the judge that he started yelling at her. His lawyer tried to calm him down, but it didn't work. At one point, the bailiff went over to his table and threatened to arrest him if he didn't stop his ranting."

"What an asshole. There's another example of why he needs to be out of your life."

"That's not all. In addition, when the judge told him that he had to give me half of his retirement account, he started screaming at his lawyer then the judge. That was it. He got arrested. Before they handcuffed him, the judge ordered him to sign the divorce agreement. As he was being removed from court, he stopped and turned toward me. He was so mad that he threatened to get back at me right there in front of the judge."

Owen shook his head in disgust, "We've got to be very careful. Don't let anyone know where you are. And, watch to see if anyone's following you."

"That's what the judge said, too. She was concerned for my safety and told me I was right to divorce him. She suggested I get a Restraining Order to keep him away from me."

"I agree with her. Do they have Family Restraining Orders?"

48

The Pool

It was the middle of the summer.

The pool at Riley's apartment was full of families with their babies and children. In the middle of the pool, away from the screaming kids, Riley and Owen floated on rubber rafts, soaking in lots of sun.

She paddled over to him and took his hand, "I just love it out here. The water feels so good."

"You've got that right. I could stay out here from morning till night. The only thing that troubles me are these kids."

"What's wrong with the kids?"

"It's Marco Polo. They're all calling for him, and they won't stop. Do you think I should tell them that Marco Polo is dead?"

Enjoying their time in the sun, they were unaware of who was about to enter the pool area.

Jase walked across the sloping grass from the apartment parking lot and stopped along the outside pool fence. He spotted Riley, turned, and headed for the entrance to the pool deck.

Once inside, he started toward his ex-wife.

Jase moved quickly over the concrete with his eyes on the center of the pool where Riley and Owen were relaxing. They both had their eyes closed.

Jase yelled at Riley, "You whore! You bitchin' whore! Get out of the pool. Now!"

Riley was first to open her eyes and looked to see that Jase was on the deck yelling at her.

She turned to Owen, "Shit! Jase is here!"

Owen got up on his elbows. Jase was not ten feet away standing on the rim of the pool with his legs wide apart.

He looked down at Owen, "You, too, asshole. Out of the pool!"

Owen was not shaken by Jase at all. He kept his cool.

He rested his head back down on the raft, closed his eyes, and called to Jase, "This is not going to go well, Jase. Go home."

Jase was hoping he could start a fight with this man twenty years older than himself, but Owen's reaction startled him. There was nothing more to say. Nothing more to do. So, Jase stood up straight and walked off the deck, slamming the gate behind him.

With a new sense of danger, Riley and Owen looked at each other. Nothing was said. Nothing had to be. Jase said it all for them.

After watching Jase walk away, Owen slid off his raft and swam underwater for a few feet. When he surfaced, Riley was just in front of him.

She looked to see that her ex-husband was out of sight, "This just keeps getting worse. I thought the divorce would end all this by now. How in Hell did he know where I live?"

"I don't know. But, like you said, he's one crazy son of a bitch."

She rested her chin on the raft and looked at Owen, "I feel like everyone's after us. There's no place safe for us."

"I think we need to disappear for a while. I'm going to call work and tell them I need to take some time off. Then you and I are going away."

"Where will we go? How long?"

"I don't know where we'll go, yet. How about Boston? I think we should go down there for a few days."

Her head snapped up, "I could do Boston for a few days. Not a problem. But, only if we stay at the Boston Harbor."

He smiled at her suggestion, "This is going to cost me a lot of money, isn't it?"

"Bet your ass it is. But, I think we deserve it. Let's get out of here."

They didn't know that someone near to them in the pool had been listening to their getaway plan.

49

The Chase

Before they drove to Boston, they dropped Zeke off at Bill Stafford's place.

Bill and his wife, Mary, didn't have any kids and entertaining Zeke for a few days was going to be a special treat for them. It also gave Owen peace of mind to know that Zeke wouldn't be in a kennel while they were away.

After saying goodbye to Zeke and the Stafford's, they drove out Sanford Road to I-95 and turned south toward Boston

They stayed on the interstate until they reached I-93 in Wakefield that would take them directly into downtown Boston.

As they neared Somerville, Owen kept glancing at his rearview mirror.

Riley noticed that his eyes had been looking at something behind them. She looked over her shoulder.

"Is there something going on behind us?"

He looked back again, "Don't worry about it. It's probably just my paranoia kicking in. But, I think we're being followed. I'm going to change our route before we get to Boston. We'll see if he follows us."

"What kind of car is it?"

"I think it's a green truck. It's about four cars back. You see it?"

Owen thought he had seen that same truck back in Wells. Whoever it was had stayed back no fewer than three cars. At first, he didn't recognize the truck at all. But then he remembered a similar truck when his tires were slashed at the Portland Airport."

Riley bent to her left and spent time examining the cars behind them, "Nope. I can't see it. It's probably just your imagination."

"Well, maybe it is. But, I'm changing course just in case."

They took the next exit onto Mystic Avenue then connected onto Route 99 through Charlestown. He checked his rearview mirror again. The green pickup was gone.

"Well, if he was following us, we lost him. He's not back there anymore."

They both relaxed with the disappearance of the truck.

They crossed the Charles River on North Washington Street.

To be sure, after they crossed the bridge into the North End, he turned right on Market Street then left on Congress.

He looked back again to be certain the truck was gone. He didn't believe what he saw.

"Shit? He's back there again."

Riley was scared, "What the fuck! Somebody really wants to scare us. What are we gonna' do?"

"Nobody knows Boston like I do. I'm going to take this asshole on a special tour of Beacon Hill. We'll lose him up there for sure."

They sped past City Hall, turned right onto State Street then continued on Court. Next, they turned left onto Tremont. After the Old Granary Burial Ground, they turned right onto Park. Then, right again onto Beacon. Then a quick left up Bowdoin past the State House. At Derne, they turned left then left again onto Hancock. They continued onto Mt. Vernon and sped down the hill. They made a sharp right into Louisburg Square and pulled into the only open space.

It was his lucky day. There was rarely an open space in Louisburg Square.

"I can't imagine that this guy's been able to keep up with us in that truck. But, just in case, we need to duck down and stay out of sight."

He adjusted his rearview mirror then crouched down as much as he could. He looked up into the mirror to see if the truck was back there looking for them. Nothing.

Riley hunched down, close to the floor.

She looked over at Owen with a shaky voice, "So, this is your idea of fun in Bean Town? I didn't know anyone could drive like that. Especially in Boston."

After several minutes went by, he checked in the mirror again. Still nothing.

"Maybe it's me, but whoever it was is not there anymore. I'm sorry to worry you like that."

Riley looked behind her seat out the back window and agreed that they were alone.

With a deep breath, she added, "Hey, listen to me. It was a little scary back there, but I'm okay now. Really. So, let's get our asses up to that luxury suite with a view. We need to rest up before we go shopping."

"Shopping? Who said anything about shopping? We're here to have some fun and get away for a while."

"You're right, Honey. That's what we're going to do. But, first we're gonna' have fun shopping!"

As they started to drive away, Riley looked out her side window at the homes in Louisburg Square and sighed, "I'd take any one of these places, thank you very much!"

Continuing through Boston's beauty, they found themselves on Atlantic Avenue. They went north past the Boston Harbor Hotel arch and turned into the Rowes Wharf Garage. They found an open space and parked the car.

Owen retrieved their lone suitcase. They walked together wheeling their bag behind them into the lobby. They checked in at the front desk.

Owen had reserved a suite overlooking the harbor. He asked a bellman to take their bag to their room and tipped him five dollars.

"Why thank you, sir. I'll take it up immediately."

After the bellman was off to their room, Riley took hold of Owen's hand, "I need a drink. How about you?"

"Good! I think I need a double."

They found two seats together in the Rowes Wharf Bar.

They had stopped talking. The look on both their faces had turned worrisome, again. They knew that their families were still fuming over what they'd done. Being divorced hadn't changed anything. In fact, it had made it worse. It was the certain end to their marriages that informed everyone it was over. There was no turning back.

Jase was still trying to decide how he might kill the two of them. The girls were outraged at their mother. Ella couldn't find a single good thing to say about her sister. Julie spent most of her time telling her friends she did nothing wrong. And, Caryn kept telling her granddaughters that their mother was a whore.

He finally spoke, "Look. I know this keeps getting worse for us. And, it's also gotten dangerous. But, I believe in us. We are free to love each other, to care for each other, to be out in the open and honest."

She took hold of both his hands, "I love you, Mr. Flynn. You know that? We're finally going to be happy with life. I'm sick of people following us, people destroying your car, people hacking your computer, people spying on us, sisters ratting on us, people threatening us, and people dying because they're my friends. If we can get past all this, we'll finally be able to live this life of ours without fear."

"We've paid a high price for what we have together. I'm never going to give you up again. Never."

Riley nodded her head then snapped back, "Speaking of high prices, let's go check out our suite then go buy something."

They jumped on an elevator that took them to their floor. After a short walk down the hall, they stopped and opened the door to their suite.

Even before they walked in, Riley looked across the spacious living room to a wall of glass through which she gasped at the entirety of Boston Harbor.

They walked toward the window, "What have you done, my love? I've never been in a room like this before."

"This is what they call the Presidential Suite. I thought you'd like to try it. There are some neat things here. Let me show you."

He walked her through the living room into the dining room. He looked back to find Riley still staring out the wall of glass. He called to get her attention and back on their tour. She didn't move at first, but then gave in.

When she entered the dining room, she was startled by the cut glass chandelier hanging over a large table with eight chairs around it. The walls were brilliant mahogany with etched, framed photos of Boston, circa 1920. The crystal glassware on the mahogany sideboard sparkled across the ceiling.

"Are we expecting any heads of state for dinner tonight?"

"Not at all. We're probably not ever going to use this room while we're here. I just thought you'd like to see it."

Before leaving the dining room, she whispered just one word, "Cute!"

He took her hand and escorted her back across the living room to the bedroom. He opened the double doors to reveal a king-size bed stacked with too many pillows to count. The room was a gorgeous light blue with gold papered walls. The carpet was plush gray and soft to the touch. There were matching gold sconces on both sides of the mahogany headboard. There was a lady's dresser for her and a man's chest of drawers for him. A mahogany desk and chair were positioned at the window, also over-looking Boston Harbor.

Without further hesitation, she walked into the bathroom and turned on the lights. She was breathless from what she saw.

Her eyes sparkled at the first thing she noticed. It was a white, French, claw-foot tub with bright chrome faucets and a hand-held shower. The back of the glazed, iron tub sloped up to support the bather's head. Next to the tub was a table that overlapped the side allowing easy access to soaps, oils, and perfumes. Or, a glass of wine.

On the other side of the bathroom was a walk-in shower. The tiled floor and walls were Travertine with a soft, cream glow to them. Riley walked in and was pleased to see that it was very large, had two benches, and two shower heads. One for each of them, preferably at the same time. The vanity was a beautiful, gray and black granite top with two sinks and a single large mirror spanning most of the wall.

When Owen joined her, she looked back over her shoulder and joked, "I guess this will do. Didn't they have anything bigger when you reserved this place?"

"Nope. This is the biggest they have. There's a reason it's called the President's Suite, ya' know?"

"Which presidents have stayed here?"

"All of them."

After a few more minutes examining the goodies around their suite, they left to go shopping.

First, they trekked over to the Boston Common then across Charles Street to the Gardens. There they caught a lazy Swan Boat before strolling down Newbury Street, the east coast version of LA's Rodeo Drive.

Riley was tickled to window shop at Burberry, Armani, Valentino, Marc Jacobs, and hours of other shops and boutiques. On occasion, she bought something 'she just had to have.'

Owen carried her bags.

Before heading back to the hotel, they stopped into the Bull & Finch Pub, better known as Cheers, on Beacon Street. They waited a few minutes for a table to open up. When they were seated, they ordered something light with a couple of Sam Adams Lagers from the tap.

As always, it was over crowded and noisy, but that's what everybody likes about Cheers.

"I love being a tourist in Boston," she yelled at Owen.

Holding his hand to his ear, he yelled back, "What was that?"

Rolling her eyes, she gave him the finger.

After they climbed the stairs back up to Beacon Street, they crossed and walked along the Boston Gardens. They crossed Charles Street and continued up the hill along the Commons. Just as they got to Joy Street, Owen stopped and grabbed her.

"What's the matter, Honey?"

"It's that pickup truck right over there. He found us!"

"What makes you think it's the same truck?"

"That truck is the same one that was in the parking garage at Portland Airport when my tires were slashed. It has that yellow stripe across the tailgate. This can't be a coincidence."

He took a strong grip on her hand and pulled her off of Beacon Street and away from the truck.

The driver was agitated watching them in his side-view mirror.

As they turned onto the sidewalk that took them diagonally across the Commons, the pickup truck spun its tires as it pulled into the traffic up Beacon Street.

Riley and Owen began to run. The truck had reached the traffic lights in front of the State House.

Almost out of breath, Owen yelled, "We need to get to the T station, the Park Street station, just ahead of us. He can't follow us down there."

"We can make it!"

As the pickup truck turned onto Park Street, the driver encountered yet more traffic lined up at the lights on Tremont.

They made it into the T Station just as the truck turned onto Tremont. The pickup slowly passed the station, but the driver couldn't find his quarry. He gave up and accelerated away.

Inside Park Street Station they took a Red Line train headed to South Station. After two stops, they got off and walked the five blocks to the hotel.

They passed through the lobby.

When they got to the bar, they sat close to each other near the windows.

Owen sat back and took a long breath, "How the Hell did this guy know we'd be there when we came out of Cheers? This is crazy!"

"I can't think straight right now. I'm scared to death."

"We never told anyone we were even going to Boston this week."

"I didn't say anything except Facebook. But, that..."

"Facebook? You posted something in Facebook about us going to Boston?"

"Before we left, all I said was that I was going to play tourist for a few days in Boston."

"That's it! This guy must have access to your Facebook wall or something. I don't have any idea how Facebook works, but he must have hacked into your account. He did a pretty good job hacking into mine. Did you say anything about the hotel?"

"No. I guess I mentioned something about drinking a Sam Adams at Cheers. I was going to post something about our suite and the shopping we just did, but I won't do that now."

"I'm going to stop at the front desk and ask them to keep our information private. I don't want him trying to find us here."

After a couple of drinks, their blood pressures calmed down. They were still scared, but the alcohol was helping a lot.

The two of them held onto each other as they passed through the lobby then up to their suite.

Once inside, Owen fell onto the bed while Riley used the bathroom. Then, she joined him on the bed.

They both fell fast asleep and had the same nightmare.

50

The Return

Riley and Owen spent their breakfast the next day talking about the truck.

She spoke first, "Who the Hell is this guy? He's got me terrified. Do you think it's Jase?"

"Not sure. He might have one of his friends after us. I can't see your ex-mother-in-law trying to pull this off. The same for Julie. How about Jase's two brothers? Yes! That's got to be who it is. They have a good reason to hurt us. They'd want to teach us a lesson to help their brother. And, they stay anonymous in that truck."

"If it is his brothers, what do we do?"

He shook his head, "There's really nothing we can do. I called the police a week ago and they told me they can't do anything unless there's a real crime committed."

"Great! So, they won't do anything to help us until we're killed. Is that it?"

"That sounds about right. Until then, we're on our own."

After three more days doing their best to enjoy as many of the touristy things they could in Boston, they drove back to Wells.

It was a somber ride. They didn't have much to say. All they could think about was the guy in the pickup truck.

Before they got to her apartment, they stopped at the Stafford's to pick up Zeke.

When they went through the door, he was there to welcome them home. His tail was wagging his love at them.

While kneeling down to pet Zeke, Owen asked, "How'd he do, Bill? Was he a good boy for you guys?"

"He sure was. We just love him. He's such a wonderful little guy."

Mary added, "He is such a lover boy. He slept with us each night and cuddled up close to both of us. We wish we had him longer. It went by too fast."

"Oh yeah? Really? I told Riley the other day that I can't keep him on the boat with me anymore. He's going nuts. He needs more space and wants to be outside a lot. I'm actually looking for someone to adopt him."

Bill looked at his wife, "This is crazy, but I think Zeke should be with us."

Mary nodded her agreement, "That would be awesome! Bill and I actually talked about him being a part of our family. He'd be our first-born son."

Owen sighed, "If you guys are okay with this, I'm okay, too. Will you let me visit with him from time to time? He loves to chase birds across the beach now and then."

Mary wrapped her arms around Zeke's neck, hugging and kissing him, "Of course! You can take him to the beach whenever you want."

Owen bent down and cupped his hands around Zeke's ears, "So, it's a deal. Zeke, my boy, you have new parents and a great big yard to play in."

Then he looked up at Bill, "He's all yours. I'll drop off his leash, harness, and all his other stuff tomorrow. He has about thirty toys at last count."

He said goodbye to Zeke with a great big, long hug. Zeke whined at them as they walked to their car.

Owen tried to wipe away his tears.

Driving back to the apartment, neither said a word. It was both a sad and a happy time for them.

When they got home, Owen parked in the guest space. He opened Riley's door then the cargo door. He grabbed their suitcase while she gathered the bags of new clothes and trinkets.

"You did the right thing. Zeke will be very happy. Bill and Mary will love him and care for him just as much as you have."

"Yeah. I know them. They'll give him a good home. And, this will be a big relief for me, too. I just couldn't give him what he needs."

When they got into Riley's apartment, Owen fell onto the couch.

Riley took her bags into the bedroom and laid them out on the bed. Happy with her purchases, she turned and headed back to the living room.

As she passed through the doorway, Owen commented, "After our suite in Boston, this apartment is suddenly much smaller now. Have you noticed?"

"Sorry. I'm not in a humorous mood right now. We have a lot to discuss."

"I'm sorry, too, Honey. Just tried to get a smile from you."

She sat on the couch close to him, put her chin in her hands, and bent down.

After a few seconds, she glanced up at him, "Are we that wrong to do this?"

"You mean, love each other like we do?"

"Yeah. Something like that. We've hurt a lot of people. Pissed off a lot of people. I don't know who this guy is, but he scares the shit out of me."

He put his arm around her neck, "Honey. Love is a test. It's to find out who we really are. Is loving one another right or wrong? Is it worth the pain it might cause? Are we better because of it? Are we helping or hurting others? There's no correct answer to any of these questions. The test is in our hearts. If we believe in who we're loving then all the answers are correct. And, we pass the test."

"How have I done? Do I pass?"

"I think you deserve an A+ for loving me. It's now a part of your record, so no one can change your grade."

They talked until midnight then went to bed. They drew close and held each other tighter than ever before.

They drifted off to sleep in each other's arms.

51

The Explosion

Owen's cell phone woke him up.

It was Bill, "Hey, buddy. Why are you calling so early?"

"I've got some really bad news, Owen."

"Uh oh. Did something happen to Zeke?"

"No. It's *Airship*. She's gone! Destroyed! I got a call from JoAnn…"

Owen jumped out of bed and screamed, "Are you shitting me? What in Hell happened?"

"Apparently it was the propane tank."

"Propane? You know as well as I do, that's not possible. We have the safest boat at the dock. There's got to be another reason for it."

"Look, Owen. I think you should get down there right away and ask these questions of the fire department. Can I meet you there in half an hour?"

"Okay. I'll be there in three minutes."

Riley was in shock as she overheard their conversation.

After he hung up, Owen sat back on the bed next to Riley. He bent his head in silence.

She put her arms around him and pulled him close, "I don't understand it. Every day it's yet another disaster."

"You know this wasn't an accident. Somebody did this to me. Just like everything else that's been going on. If it's Jase, I'm going after him. I swear this is going to stop if it kills me."

Owen got dressed and raced to his car. Riley barely got ready as she tried to keep up with him. The two jumped in and sped off for the marina.

When they arrived, it was just before 7:00. A cleanup crew from the fire department was doing its best to put out what remained of the fire.

The fire marshal was there directing his team. Owen approached him and introduced himself.

"I assume that you're the fire marshal?"

"Yes, that's correct. I'm Paul Langley. Are you Mr. Flynn?"

"Yes. I am. What happened here?"

He looked at his clipboard then read some of the notes off the sheet of paper, "At about 3:10 this morning, witnesses reported an explosion on your boat. Even though she was a big boat, she went down fast. It tore the shit... excuse me..., the crap out of the hull. No one was onboard. No one saw anyone snooping around her either. But, so far, we've asked more questions than we've gotten answers. This may take a week or so before we have anything to go on.

I do need to ask you some questions, though. First off, where were you around 3:00 this morning?"

Looking at Riley, "I was with Miss Reed, here, in her apartment."

Riley confirmed it, "That's right. He was with me all night."

The fire marshal nodded at her then asked, "Okay. So, what kind of insurance do you have on your boat?"

"Just the standard policy for the value of the boat. Nothing higher. I can get you the policy later today."

"Yes, we'll need to see that. Can you tell me the last time you had a party onboard your boat?"

He looked at Riley, "Never. I've never had a party on her, ever. She was a racing boat. I sailed her in competition or out all by myself. Other than that, I've had two, maybe three, people aboard at the most."

"Can I get a list of the people who've been out with you?"

"Of course. I'll get that to you as well. Can I ask you something?"

"Of course, sir. What is it?"

He chose his words carefully, "Could this have been deliberate? Maybe arson?"

"That relates to my next question. Is anyone trying to hurt you, Mr. Flynn?"

Bill arrived and joined Owen and Riley with the fire Marshall, "Hi, I'm Bill Stafford. I'm a good friend of Mr. Flynn and a crew member aboard his boat. Can I help answer any questions?"

The fire marshal changed to a clean page then asked Bill, "Where were you when Mr. Flynn's boat exploded?"

"I was home with my family. We were planning to spend the day at the beach. A friend called and woke me up to tell me what happened. Suffice it to say, it changed our plans for the day completely."

"Who was the friend who called you?"

"It was another one of our crew members. She and her husband live here in Wells and were on their boat when this happened. Her name is JoAnn Higgins. She is, or was, one of our rail huggers."

"I know Mrs. Higgins. I'll give her a call."

After a few more questions, the marshal turned to leave when he stopped and looked back at Owen.

"It's a damn good thing you weren't onboard, Mr. Flynn. This would be a murder investigation instead of just a case of arson."

Riley and Owen looked at each other. They both tried to digest what they'd just heard. Was this related to that guy in the green pickup truck again? Was it the families again? It had to be Jase.

The three of them walked down to the burned dock to get as good a look at *Airship* as they could.

One of the fire crew called out to them, "Watch out there. The dock is pretty bad and might give way if you get too close to the edge."

Bill waved at him and agreed, "Thanks! We'll stay as far away as we can. I don't plan on going for a swim right now."

When they got to a point where they could see what was left of *Airship*, they were aghast. The entire upper deck was gone and floating in pieces all around the docks and boats at berth in the marina. The outline of the hull could barely be seen a few feet under water. The mast lay in the grass next to the parking lot. Her sails, stays, and lines were entangled around it. Some of the other boats nearby had been damaged in the blast.

Riley started to cry.

They walked off the dock and onto the grass.

Owen stopped and asked her, "Why are they so determined to hurt us? Just because we fell in love? Because they feel pain? Where is the understanding? Where is the forgiveness? Where is the acceptance?

We're not evil monsters who set out to hurt everyone."

52

The Cancer

Just then, Owen staggered.

He was dizzy. Very dizzy.

Riley grabbed ahold of his left arm to steady him. Bill took hold of his right.

At first, Riley assumed he had stumbled on a rock. But, the ground where he was standing was only smooth grass. There were no rocks that could have caused the problem.

Owen was weak. He wanted to lie down for a while. They eased him onto the grass. He looked into the morning sun and closed his eyes.

Riley knelt down to him, "You okay there, mister?"

"Yeah. I think so. I'll be all right in a few minutes."

Something was going on in his brain. It was very troubling and had been bothering him for months. When it started getting worse, he didn't tell Riley about it. He didn't want her to worry.

After a while, he was able to straighten up. With a little more help from Bill and Riley, they got him to his car. He climbed into the passenger seat. Riley took the controls.

On the way back to her apartment, she told him, "I think you need to see a doctor. When was your last checkup?"

He lied to her, "I saw my VA doctor about six months ago. She didn't tell me there was anything to worry about."

When they reached her apartment, Riley helped him out of the car and up to her apartment.

With Owen's bed at the bottom of the marina, Riley told him, "I always knew we'd eventually be living together. I just didn't think it would be this way. Are you okay moving in with me now?"

"I feel like I've been living with you already. It's a good thing I don't snore."

"If you did, you'd be living out of the backseat of your car."

They laughed then laid down together on her bed.

"Riley? Honey? We've been through much more than any couple deserves. Life doesn't owe us anything. We've fought hard for everything we have. And, it's wonderful. I know I tell you every day that I love you. Now I want you to know that this love of ours is bigger, much bigger, than anything I'd ever wished it could be. That's because of you. You aren't just gorgeous. You're beautiful beyond words. You're sexy as Hell. You're delicate and soft. But, you're tough when you need to be. You have a sense of what's around you when everyone else is clueless. You're smarter than I am, and you have a wonderful wit. You can be funny and sad at the same time. You know how to make people laugh or cry. You make friendships that last a lifetime. And, you know how to love completely. I wish I was just one-tenth the person you are. But, I'll never be."

"Are you trying to hit on me?"

"Damn! Was it that obvious?"

They wrapped their arms around each other and rolled across the bed. They stopped and kissed. They kissed a lot.

He looked at her, "I meant everything I just said about you. I wish I could live the rest of my life with you. You've made me forever happy. But, there will come a time when this will end."

"What the fuck are you talking about?"

With sadness in his eyes, he explained, "Let's remember I'm twenty-five years older than you. I'm older than your father was, and he's not with us anymore. I take more medications each day than you take in five years. I'm not getting any younger, and I'm not getting any healthier. I keep telling you to go out there and find Charlie. He's looking for you. And, he'll take really good care of you."

Sharing his sadness, she asked, "Where are you going with this? You're scaring me."

"I don't mean to scare you. I've always wanted to keep you safe and to make you as happy as humanly possible. I think I've done a good job of that. But, there are things going on that scare me, too."

"What have I done wrong?"

"You've not done anything wrong at all. It's me. For some time now, I've been sick. I didn't want to tell you before this, but I have to, now."

"My God, Owen. Honey? What is it?"

"At first, I was hoping it would just go away, but it got worse. My doctors at the VA told me that it's because of Agent Orange. You don't know what that was. You're too young to know. It was used in Vietnam, and I was exposed to a lot of it."

"So, how do they fix it?"

"No, Honey, they can't. It's a rare form of cancer. My doctors want me to check into the VA hospital up in Lewiston. But, I want to stay here with you."

"Yes! I can take care of you right here. I'll get someone to run the salon for me, and I'll be here every minute. I'll get you the medications and the doctors you need. You'll get better. I'll make you better! You'll see!"

"You are my life, Riley. I don't know how this is going to go. I don't know how long I have. But, staying here with you will be my greatest joy! And, when I die, I want to be in your arms."

Riley shook her head, "Listen to me, now, and listen good. That's the last time we will ever talk about dying around here. Got it?"

Owen tried to smile at her, "Yes, Ma'am. From now on, we'll only talk about living. I promise."

53

The Girls

A week later, Owen retired from United Airlines.

His coworkers gave him a rousing sendoff. All of the senior management and staff at the airport were there. Even Sergeant Belmont.

Of course, Riley was there, too. She had a wonderful time meeting Owen's 'airport family.' It was fun to hear all the stories about him and the 'many mistakes' he'd made on the job. But mostly, people told her how much they enjoyed working with him over his twenty years at United.

As the time wound down, Owen told Riley, "I need to say a few words to thank everyone. Come with me."

He took her hand and together they walked to the microphone in front of the windows, "Hey, everybody. Before you all start to take off, so to speak, I want to express my appreciation to all of you for this magnificent party. Frankly, I didn't deserve it. There are a lot of bad things I could tell you about me to prove it."

Someone called out to him, "Not a problem, Owen. We already knew you used to rob banks."

Everyone nodded in agreement… and laughed.

Owen smiled and continued, "Okay. Okay. That's enough of that. I need to get serious now. Let me say that in my career I've been fortunate to have had the opportunity to work with some really great people. All of us here at United chose to be part of this awesome company. They hire only the best here, and you are all solid evidence of that! It troubles me to say goodbye to you all. I wish you all great success. Thank you so very much for all you've done for me over these many years."

Everyone in the crowd applauded. Many wiped tears from their eyes. They all took time to say their goodbyes to Owen and Riley.

While driving back to the apartment, Riley told him, "Did you know that these people loved you so much? I talked with a lot of them, and they told me so many wonderful things about you. But, mostly, they appreciated your leadership and the respect you showed to everyone. I'm very proud of you, mister."

"Well, they said those things to you because I made certain only the happy people were invited."

They laughed together then she added, "I don't believe that, not for one minute. Owen, Honey, I fell in love with a very special man. And, all these people told me about the wonderful goodness in you."

"I'll bet none of them ever talked with your ex-husband or your daughters about me. They'd have a very different going away party for me."

Just after they got back to the apartment, Owen went into the bedroom to change his clothes.

Riley's phone rang, "Hello?"

"Ma. It's me."

Riley straightened up when she heard her daughter, "Lauren? It's so good to hear from you, sweetie! Do I hear you crying? Is everything all right?"

"No. Everything's not all right. It's Dad."

Riley walked her phone into the bathroom and closed the door, "What is it? What's happened?"

"He beat the crap out of Craig, Kelly's boyfriend."

"What!? Why in Hell did he do that?"

"All I know is that Craig and Kelly were in her room smoking pot. And,..."

"Oh, no! I can guess the rest. Your father has been very strict about drugs. You know that, right?"

"Yes, of course. But, Kelly thought they could get away with it. I guess, Dad could smell it in the hallway. Anyway, we had to call an ambulance to take Craig to the hospital. Dad wouldn't stop punching him. He was still unconscious when they came for him. The police are here, too."

Riley was speechless, at first. She wasn't sure what to say to her daughter.

Then she tried to calm her Lauren down, "Sweetie, are you guys going to be okay? Want me to come get you?"

"Yes, Ma. We need to get out of here. Can you come soon?"

"I'm on my way."

After she hung up, she yelled to Owen as she ran out the door, "Honey, my girls are having a problem at home. I've got to get over there right away. I'll call you from the road."

"Okay, Honey. I'll see you when you get back. Stay safe."

Riley called Owen from her car.

Owen answered, "So, what's going on?"

"It's Jase. Apparently, he beat the shit out of Kelly's boyfriend. They had to get him to the hospital. The police are at the house now. I'm on my way to get the girls out of there."

Riley sped to her ex-husbands house, *"That sonofabitch! Now he's hurting our daughters?"*

When she pulled up in their driveway, Riley called Lauren's phone, "Okay. I'm here. Don't tell your Dad. Just get in my car. I'm taking you two to my apartment."

Lauren and Kelly flew out of their house and into Riley's backseat. They were crying hard.

Kelly told her mother, "I left a note in the kitchen for Dad. I told him we were going to stay with a friend and will call him later."

"Good idea, Kelly. We don't want to create any more problems with your father."

Riley sped out of the driveway and onto the road to her apartment.

Lauren spoke up, "We have to talk, Ma."

Riley pulled into her space in the parking lot. When they entered the apartment, Owen was waiting for them on the couch. He stood up to great them.

"Girls, this is Owen Flynn. Owen, this is Kelly and that's Lauren."

Lauren was first to shake his hand. She felt uncomfortable at first.

Next, Kelly gave him a modest smile and said, "Hello, again. I believe we've spoken over the phone before?"

"That we did. It's very nice to finally meet the two of you. Your mother never stops talking about you. She loves you guys very much."

The girls were speechless.

Owen continued, "I'm sorry, but I've got some work to do. So, I'm going to leave you guys alone. Let me know if you need anything."

He went to the master bedroom and closed the door.

Riley asked the girls to sit next to her on the couch, "Come join me. Let's talk."

Kelly spoke first, "We've been having a lot of problems with Dad. Tonight was definitely the worst that it's been."

Lauren jumped in, "I think we're seeing the problems you had with Dad, Ma. I mean, he controls us all the time, now. We can't even go out without him asking us a hundred questions. And,..."

Kelly interrupted, "And, he calls us all the time to find out where we are and what we're doing. It's embarrassing! I can't stand it, Ma. And, tonight he tried to kill my boyfriend?"

Riley tried to find the right words before she reacted to what she'd just heard. Her children were scared. They were angry at their father. They'd been told so many bad things about their mother. They heard it from their father, their aunt, and their grandmother for so long. They finally saw that it wasn't true. None of it.

Riley found the words, "Living with your father was a constant nightmare. I'm sorry that I had to lie to you. Instead of lying, I should have divorced him early on and taken the two of you with me. But, I was scared. Then I met Owen. I want so much for you to treat him well. He's done nothing wrong, except fall in love with me. He keeps me safe. He trusts me.

He takes wonderful care of me. He loves me completely, and we are going to be together forever. And, Owen did not, I repeat, did not steal me away from your father. That's absurd. Instead, your father pushed me away from him. Do you see it now? And, by the way, I am not a whore!"

The girls got up and hugged their mother from both sides.

Kelly admitted, "Yes, Ma. I'm so sorry for being such a bitch to you. Just be patient with me. It will take some time for me to accept... our situation."

Lauren added, "Me, too, Ma. I'm so sorry."

Riley called out to Owen, "Hey, Honey? Can you come sit with us?"

Owen left the bedroom and sat down with Riley and the girls. They talked together long into the night. The tension and anxiety left them all.

Lauren explained, "Ma, we can't go back to the house. We won't go back."

Their mother agreed, "Then you must stay here with us! You'll have to share a bed until I buy a house. Besides, I'm pretty sure that, by then, you two will be off getting married."

Everyone laughed. The two girls hung their arms around Riley and squeezed her tight.

Later, the girls climbed into their new bed. Riley and Owen settled into theirs.

They all enjoyed their first peaceful night in years.

54

The End

Present day…

Riley finished telling her story to Charlie, "So, you met my daughters a while ago. They've been with me ever since that night.

Owen left for the hospital three months later. I tried to visit him there as often as I could. It didn't take long before I could see that he was worn out and ready to die. It was awful. Thank God you came into my life when I needed you most."

Charlie didn't say a word. He didn't have to.

They got up off the bench and moved out the door of the chapel. It was 3:00 and the sky was bright and cloudless. They were holding hands. Riley cried softly.

He stopped her and took hold of both her hands, "Thanks for telling me about you and Owen. I'm amazed, frankly, that all that happened to you."

"So am I. But, I had Owen with me all the time. He really helped me get through it."

"Did you ever find out who it was who terrorized the two of you?"

"No. We never found out who it was. To this day, I really believe it was my ex-husband, but we couldn't prove it."

He kissed her hand, "I'm sorry you had to go through all that. Nevertheless, somehow Owen knew that you and I would find each other."

Riley agreed, "As I said, he wanted you to be a better man than he was. He predicted that you'd be younger, smarter, healthier, and more handsome. He also knew that you'd have green eyes, just like his."

Wincing at the sun, Charlie disagreed, "Except for the green eyes, I'm not sure that I meet the criteria he wanted for you."

She put her arms around him and kissed him, "I think he got it just about right."

He pulled back a little, "There's one thing I noticed during the ceremony that I need to ask you."

"What's that?"

"You told me about the love codes that you and Owen used. I thought you'd told me all of them, but your flower arrangement inside had on it 3-1-6-3. I couldn't figure it out. What does it stand for?"

She laughed, "I was wondering if you'd notice it. You remember 1-4-3?"

"Of course. That one's easy. It means, 'I love you.'"

"Well, early in my affair with Owen, we were parked behind the shopping center. I handed him a card with '1-4-3 – 3-1-6-3' in it. When he opened the card, he spent a lot of time trying to figure out the second part of the code. He just couldn't.

So, I said to him, '*What's wrong with you? That's so easy.*'

Then he explained, '*I think I got the first part right. Is it, 'and I always'? I just can't figure out the three-letter word at the end.*'"

Riley laughed again, "So, I grabbed the card from him, took a look at what I'd written, and was shocked at what I saw. I had miscounted the number of letters in the last word. From that day on, we always signed our notes '1-4-3, 3-1-6-3' which meant..."

Before she could finish, a green pickup truck raced up the empty drive heading toward them. Charlie pulled Riley out of the way just as the truck sped toward her.

It flew past, stopped at the Commitment Center, and turned around. The driver gunned the engine then started back toward them.

Riley was in shock and couldn't move.

Charlie was startled at what had just happened, *"Not the green pickup truck? Who the fuck is this guy?"*

He yelled at Riley, "Get out of the way! I think he wants to run us over."

Riley quickly turned and jumped through her passenger door. She opened the glove compartment and pulled out Owen's Glock. She pushed a full magazine into the handle and cocked a round into the chamber.

She stepped into the road and wrapped both hands around the gun. She spread her feet apart and pointed the gun at the truck speeding toward her. She was steady and determined.

The driver of the truck never knew that Riley had just fired off three quick rounds through his windshield. Two of them destroyed his skull.

With its driver dead, the truck veered off the pavement. It missed Riley by only two feet as it careened past her. Then, it slammed into one of the trees lining the road.

The two of them approached the damaged truck. Just in case, Riley kept her pistol pointed at the driver. Smoke began to rise from the broken engine.

The driver's door had sprung open when the truck hit the tree. The body inside was laying across the seat. His head and shoulders were covered in blood.

"Oh my God, Charlie! What the Hell is going on here? Who is that? Is it Jase?"

Charlie got closer to the driver. He checked the driver's pulse and confirmed that he was dead. The driver's wallet was sticking out of his back pocket. Charlie grabbed it and pulled out the driver's license.

Riley couldn't control her emotions and demanded, "Who is this creep?"

Charlie checked the name and address then read it to her, "His name is Daniel McGregor from Portland."

Riley lowered her pistol and couldn't believe what she'd just heard, "Jesus, Charlie! Daniel McGregor? That's Danny! You know? He was the guy I told you molested me when I was little?"

"Holly shit! I thought you told me he was in prison."

"He was. But, remember how Colleen whispered something to me before we left the funeral today? Well, she told me she'd heard that McGregor had been set free and came back to town years ago. She told me to watch out for him. I guess she was right. I was always worried that he'd try to hurt me after what I told the judge what he did to Annie and me."

Charlie put his arms around her, "So, he's the one who did all those things to you and Owen?"

"It has to be. He must have killed Viv. And, slashed Owen's tires, smashed his car windows, tried to run us down in Boston, and destroyed Owen's boat!"

Charlie added, "This guy was completely deranged. It's as simple as that. I'll bet he wanted to get his revenge from you for being sent to prison, and he came pretty damn close to doing it. I better call 9-1-1. I think we'll be here for a while."

Charlie got on his cell phone. Riley leaned against the car and looked up at the Commitment Center.

Her thoughts turned to Owen, *"I'm so sorry, Owen. We paid a very high price for our love. But, it was worth every second of it. Thank you for what you did for me. You're the very best part of me, now. I will never forget you. Never! Rest in peace, my love. Stay safe. I love you…,*

and I always wil."

www.ingramcontent.com/pod-product-compliance
Lightning Source LLC
LaVergne TN
LVHW011217080426
835509LV00005B/183